Overcoming

Rejection

"TRIUMPHING OVER

IT'S CHALLENGES"

By Bradley Stuart

ISBN: 978-0-9976893-2-7

DEDICATION

I want to dedicate this book to my family, who have walked through my rejection challenges and been patient with me as I have worked through them.

I want to dedicate it to my wife, who has been willing to help me as I've walked through these challenges. Instead of rejecting me, she encouraged and enabled me to work through them.

I want to dedicate it to my faithful friends who have cheered me on to write the life lessons they have learned that have helped them overcome their rejection challenges.

ACKNOWLEDGMENT

I want to thank my wife for all her patience in helping me work through my rejection challenges without rejecting me. With her help and patience, I am writing this book. I will be ever grateful, and so will you, for her encouraging me to not only see the negative aspects of my rejection challenges. Her encouragement to look for positive life lessons instead of just seeing the negative ones changed my life and I am convinced it will change yours, too. I am learning not to look at lemons (my rejection challenges) as something bitter but to see their positive potential. This mindset changed everything for me, and I'm convinced it will for you, too.

Our rejection challenges can be viewed negatively, causing pain and making us tough and bitter. Alternatively, they can be seen as opportunities to become tender and better rather than allowing them to affect our attitudes towards ourselves and others negatively. Instead of allowing our rejection and challenges to be stumbling blocks holding us back, we can start seeing them as positive lessons to help us see ourselves and others correctly. Helping others, we see them as some of the most constructive building blocks we can use to build our lives.

Thanks to my wife, Sue, through this book, I will discuss how to remove your rejection-filtered glasses. As they make, you see all your life experiences negatively. I will help you put on fresh glasses of acceptance. Your new glasses of acceptance will not stop you from rejection. However, they will help you filter what you see and think about yourself and others. Your new perspective will help you see how many lemonade varieties you can make with your lemons. I will take you on a journey to show you how many building blocks you have to help others through the rejection you have experienced. I will discuss twenty varieties of lemonade I have discovered through my life experiences. These experiences have allowed me to see my life as a journey filled with rejection challenges I've had to overcome. My changed perspective helped me go from feeling like a victim to seeing myself as someone who has triumphed over my rejection challenges. With each triumphant victory gained, I have grown to understand and know how to work through the challenge. Taking what I've learned to help others do the same.

Are you up for seeing which rejection challenges you may have already triumphed over and which ones you are facing? Finally, how can your understanding equip you to help those around you stuck on their rejection journey?

ABOUT THE AUTHOR

Bradley Stuart was born and raised in South Africa. Because of many problems at the time of his birth, doctors finally diagnosed Bradley with cerebral palsy at four. Bradley attended a particular school for those with cerebral palsy for four years. He then started attending a regular public school. Academically, Bradley did well. However, emotionally, he began being teased and bullied, as children rejected him for being handicapped. They called him all kinds of derogatory names and made fun of him continually.

In this book, Bradley will share his journey of overcoming twenty challenges rooted in rejection. As Bradley started triumphing over these rejection challenges and talking to others about them, he found how helpful they were to others. Therefore, he began teaching them as he lived them out. He eventually used his insights into rejection challenges to help people in more than thirty countries.

Bradley has been so encouraged by how his insights have helped him and how they have helped others he has put them into writing.

TABLE OF CONTENTS

INTRODUCTION
"OVERCOMING REJECTION
CHALLENGES"

"I'm sorry to say that your son didn't make it, and I apologize for delivering this news after all the hard labor and travail. He is not breathing."

"No, help!" My mother cried out, "Help!" And then a miracle happened.

A doctor in training walked in, raised me from the dead, and placed me in an incubator. However, the challenges did not stop there. In the incubator, I got yellow jaundice and pneumonia. The challenges continued when a nurse injected me with a dirty needle. I began hemorrhaging, and the doctor gave me only two hours to live. But amazingly, I made it through that challenge and lived.

At four, they finally diagnosed me with cerebral palsy, and my parents were told I might never walk or talk. After four years of being helped at a particular school for disabled students, I attended a regular public school. My classmates constantly teased and challenged me because of my handicap.

I have identified four primary reactions to rejection challenges:

INTRODUCTION

1. Fear:

° Fear is a typical initial emotional response when faced with rejection challenges. It's a natural reaction to uncertainty or perceived threats.

° Consequences: Fear can paralyze individuals, preventing them from taking action or making rational decisions. It may lead to avoidance or procrastination, hindering personal and professional growth.

2. Panic:

° Panic is an intense and often irrational reaction to challenging situations. It can involve heightened anxiety and a sense of losing control.

° Consequences: Panic can lead to impulsive decisions or erratic behavior, which may exacerbate the problem. It can also negatively impact mental and physical health.

3. Over-Analyzing:

° Some people respond to challenges by becoming hyper-vigilant and overly focused on details. They may analyze the situation excessively.

° Consequences: While attention to detail is essential, over-analyzing can lead to analysis paralysis. This can delay progress and hinder problem-solving by getting lost in minor details.

4. *Wrong Attitudes:*

○ This reaction suggests that individuals may approach challenges with negative attitudes, such as pessimism, cynicism, or defeatism.

○ Consequences: A negative attitude can become a self-fulfilling prophecy. It can prevent individuals from seeing opportunities within challenges and hinder creative problem-solving.

I never had a guide to show me how to identify or cope with my twenty adverse reactions to my rejection challenges. By reading this book, I can show how to recognize and cope with each one. I will show you how they break us down, how to gain breakthroughs, and finally, how we can positively inspire those around us through our breakthroughs. Are you ready to visit these twenty rejection challenges most of us face, knowing or unknowing? Overcoming these will make you feel triumphant and help you enable those around you to become triumphant, too.

Despite all of my rejection challenges, I graduated from high school. I got my Ph.D. Summa Cum Laude and have traveled to thirty-eight nations helping people to overcome their rejection challenges.

INTRODUCTION

Definition of Challenges:

(The situation being faced with) Something that needs great mental or physical effort to be done successfully and, therefore, tests a person's ability.[1]

Why you need to read this book:

Rejection challenges are an inherent aspect of our daily lives. They can trigger various emotional responses, such as fear, worry, anger, and the tendency to avoid them. These emotions significantly affect our ability to function effectively and overcome challenges.

What you'll gain from reading this book:

We all face rejection challenges daily; some are more obvious than others. Overcoming these rejection challenges made me learn to become triumphant when meeting mine. Overcoming my rejection challenges changed my life, and it can change yours, too.

Here are the twenty rejection challenges I would like to help you overcome in your life and the lives of others:

1. Communication Breakdown - Putting up walls of self-protection to protect ourselves and affecting our communication with others and theirs with us.

Are there walls to be broken down by you or those around you?

---

[1] 1 https://dictionary.cambridge.org/us/dictionary/english/challenge

2. Distant and Edgy—Fears cause us to become distant and edgy. Fearful and edgy affect our boldness and confidence.

Do you find yourself distant and edgy toward others or others toward you, affecting your boldness and confidence?

3. People Pleasers - A lack of boundaries causes us not to say no. We become bitter, resentful, and angry by taking on too much.

How easy is it for you to say no? Do you find others always saying yes?

4. Controlling Relationships - We give ourselves to others and allow them to control us. Control destroys relationships.

Can you set clear boundaries with others, and can they set clear boundaries with you?

5. Driven—Overperforming for acceptance and approval. Feeling like "human doings" instead of "human beings," we lack motivation.

Why are you doing what you are doing, and why are others around you doing what they are doing?

6. Forceful Actions and Reactions - Becoming destructive causes conflict and rebellion.

Are you someone who uses force to get what you want, or are you often subject to others' forceful control?

7. Overpowering and Manipulative—We become overpowering by misusing our strengths and capabilities, which leads to manipulation and abuse of others.

Do you use your strengths and capabilities to manipulate others, or do others control you?

8. Controlling Through Silence—We use silent defiance to get others to respond to us, and our silent defiance destroys our relationships.

Do you use silent defiance to control others, or do they use it to control you?

9. Constant Conflict - Resisting any authority causes continuous conflict with others. Therefore, lacking the power to lead correctly.

How do you or others respond to those in authority? How do others react to your authority?

10. Unteachable - Retaliating negatively to any correction. Retaliation results in stunted growth and effectiveness.

Are you open to being corrected, and how do others respond when you try to correct them?

11. Disdainful - Feelings of worthlessness and undervalued. Affecting our motivation, effectiveness, and relationships.

What is your self-talk like, and how do you find others around you talking about themselves?

12. Lack of confidence - Focusing primarily on our weaknesses instead of our strengths can lead to feelings of self-pity.

What attitude do you have about yourself, and what are those around you saying about your efforts?

13. Unmotivated - Denying we have anything of value to contribute to others, we become selfish. Selfishness causes shame and guilt.

How free are you in giving what you have to others, and how willing are others to provide what they have to you?

14. Isolated and Distant - Insecurity and shyness lead to isolation, criticism, and a judgmental attitude.

How bold are you around others, and how bold are they around you?

15. Procrastinating and Retreating—Our fear of making mistakes makes us retreat instead of advance, preventing us from learning great life lessons.

How do you respond to your mistakes, and how do those you are around view their mistakes?

16. Bitter and Resentful - Being bitter and resentful towards others' reactions defiles our attitudes.

Have you allowed others' actions or reactions to you to cause bitterness to grow, or have others around you become bitter?

17. Uncooperative - Rejecting others for rejecting us creates a vicious cycle of painful rejection.

INTRODUCTION

Do you reject those who reject you or see others rejecting people around you?

18. Hypersensitive - Hypersensitive and reacting to specific triggers make us feel vulnerable or hurt.

What actions or reactions are you most sensitive to, and who do you find super sensitive to you?

19. Distant and Selfish - Selfishly withholding information we should be sharing and fearing rejection if we get engaged.

How willing are you to give what you have to those unfamiliar, and how willingly do others share what they have with you?

20. Wanting Perfection - Fear of rejection if we don't do things ideally causes a judgmental mindset.

Do you find yourself driven to do things perfectly, and what attitude do others have as they work with you?

Can you identify with these rejection challenges or know someone who can? I want to offer practical, proven, real-life solutions. These proven real-life solutions have empowered me to identify what was behind my adverse reactions. By discussing my rejection challenges. I hope to provide real-life solutions to make you and those around you more invincible. You may say: "Why can you be so confident? In the past thirty years of teaching, I have witnessed definite positive outcomes in the lives of those I've helped and trained to assist others.

OVERCOMING REJECTION

Overcoming rejection challenges is almost impossible when you don't get practical help or guidance. Will you allow me to be your guide and lead you in overcoming your rejection challenges? Or to better equip you to help others facing rejection challenges around you? I will show you how to recognize and start overcoming twenty rejection challenges. A process that took me years to identify and overcome. With the insights I have to share, I am convinced you will begin overcoming your rejection challenges more speedily than I did. As you overcome your rejection challenges, you will help others to do the same if they are willing.

Recognizing these twenty rejection challenges takes time, as it is not an instant event but an ongoing journey of discovery. It took much longer to realize my rejection challenges, as many had become second nature. I only briefly looked for positive results from my challenges, which held me back. This continued until my wife encouraged me to look at what I could see positively instead of staying focused on the negative aspects. My wife challenged me to make lemonade with the lemons (rejection challenges) I had in my hand. This was a huge step forward for me. It opened up a new way of approaching my rejection challenges. As I did this, I realized every negative challenge could produce a positive effect. It radically changed my attitude and my approach to my rejection challenges. My attitude change caused a mindset change, profoundly affecting my actions and reactions. I turned my stumbling blocks into building blocks by changing my negative attitude and focus.

INTRODUCTION

When we face rejection challenges, we either become passive or aggressive in our response. Both reactions lead to angry aggression. Researchers identify this as the fight-or-flight reaction. Fear triggers both responses.[2]

PRACTICALLY APPROACHING

OUR REJECTION CHALLENGES:

I created a three-step process to deal with my rejection challenges, turning them into opportunities.

- **First**, **breakdowns** cause negative attitudes, actions, and reactions.

- **Second,** we need **breakthroughs** to change the cycle and overcome them.

- **Third**, we see how we can **inspire** others through our breakthroughs.

These steps helped me overcome each rejection challenge, making lemonade from my lemons.

---

[2] MSEd, K. C. (2022, November 7). *What is the Fight-or-Flight response?* Verywell Mind. https://www.verywellmind.com/what-is-the-fight-or-flight-response-2795194

REPEATED PATTERNS

Patterns you need to recognize and master:

When challenged, we become **frustrated and angry** when we can't effectively overcome our rejection challenges. Depending on our maturity level, this can result in internal frustration and tears to release how we feel. Tears and anger can lead to emotional control.

We may use **domination, intimidation, or manipulation** to avoid getting hurt. However, this control overrides others' free will.

We need to find out the root of our rejection challenges. Procrastination hinders us from our breakthrough. Getting to the root requires patience, a quality many of us need to improve in our microwave society. This process can be messy and painful, demanding honesty, humility, and a teachable heart.

*** Throughout this book, when I talk about father figures, you could also use a mother figure if this applies to you

SECTION ONE

FEAR

CHAPTER ONE

THE CHALLENGE OF WALLS

I sat alone in my room on a Friday night, thinking about the weekend. I felt a sinking feeling of loneliness in the pit of my stomach. Why?

My father had many projects to finish and would be working on. My stepmother would work two 12-hour shifts in the local emergency room. The only people I had to look forward to spending time with were our domestic maid and my younger siblings.

Sitting there that night, realizing how painful this place of isolation had become, I knew things had to change. My desperation led me to ask myself some hard questions. Through this, I discovered much of what I was feeling was because of the walls of self-protection I had built around myself. Why was I in this prison of self-isolation?

It was my way of protecting myself from the unique, painful rejection challenges I received from those around me who did not understand why I walked and talked the way I did. My cerebral palsy made it harder for me to function as freely as others around me could function. Seeing my adverse reactions to my cerebral palsy was extremely painful. Therefore, I protected myself by building walls of self-protection. However, I slowly realized that these walls hurt me more than they protected me.

BREAKDOWN

When faced with rejection challenges, we become driven by fear, building walls of self-protection around ourselves. Our self-protective walls result in:

PROFOUNDLY AFFECTING OUR RELATIONSHIPS

Unresolved emotional issues and pain have a profound and lasting effect on our relationships. These hidden challenges can create ongoing turmoil and strain.

EVASION OF PAIN

Human nature compels us to avoid confronting emotional pain directly, leading us to employ various avoidance strategies. These avoidance behaviors hinder our ability to acknowledge and effectively cope with our pain, leaving us trapped in a cycle of discomfort.

INVESTMENT IN SELF-PROTECTIVE WALLS

The considerable time and energy spent constructing and maintaining emotional self-protective walls can be counterproductive. These defenses shield us from potential harm but, paradoxically, can isolate us from growth, connection, and personal development. This diverts resources away from meaningful pursuits. Breaking down these walls leads to a more fulfilling and authentic existence.

The fight-or-flight response is a fundamental survival mechanism hard-wired into our biology to help us deal with immediate threats. However, as you rightly pointed out, this response can also manifest in counterproductive ways when facing personal challenges. This is especially true in the areas of personal growth and development.

Building walls around oneself, whether physical or metaphorical, has been a common strategy throughout history to protect against external threats. With cities building walls, this was a practical way to defend against invading armies or other dangers. Similarly, on a personal level, individuals often build walls to shield themselves from fear, rejection, or hurt. These walls can be emotional barriers, avoidance behaviors, or defensive attitudes.

While such self-protective mechanisms can be helpful in the short term, they can also hinder personal growth and damage relationships in the long run.

We feel safer behind our walls of self-protection, as our walls create a false sense of security. Our false sense of comfort or security deceives us into thinking, "Yes, I've done it! They cannot penetrate and hurt me anymore!" As we settle down in our false comfort zone for a season, the pain seems to disappear, but sadly, another pain rears its head and plagues us. The pain of lonely self-isolation takes over, causing even deeper pain than our rejection challenges did.

The cruelest form of punishment, besides corporal punishment, is solitary confinement. We are all to be in relationships with others, starting with our mother right after birth. After bonding correctly with our mothers, we should bond with our fathers, family, friends, and co-workers. The prison of self-isolation is a tough place to be in. If we don't connect with our mothers enough at birth, it can affect our future relationships and lives. Many articles show how a lack of mother-child bonding affects adult relationships later.[3]

In addition, a lack of bonding profoundly affects orphans. As we fear rejection from others, we choose to self-isolate and feel lonely. In short, our isolation can bring harmful consequences.

Our prison walls hurt our ability to build the relationships we should build with others. These relationships should enrich our lives, making us most effective at what we should do for and with others. Rejecting those who can teach us valuable life lessons results from building walls around ourselves. We should open up and be honest about how we perceive others are making us feel, but we choose to run from them instead. We become more vulnerable to bitterness and resentment if we dwell on our selfish thoughts and emotions.

The more that bitterness and resentment grow, the more we drive those we should be in relationships with from our lives. We rationalize our pattern of driving people away from ourselves by thinking, "Yes. I did it again. I avoided interaction with them, preventing them from hurting me." However, a few hours later, we only think: "Why am I feeling so isolated, alone, and down?" We do not realize we are in a prison of our own making created by our fear-based decisions.

---

[3] Winston, R., & Chicot, R. (2016b). The importance of early bonding on the long-term mental health and resilience of children. *London Journal of Primary Care*, 8(1), 12–14. https://doi.org/10.1080/17571472.2015.1133012

Our fears often lead us to avoid building and maintaining relationships. Our avoidance compels us to confront rejection challenges and make complex changes, regardless of the outcome. It's essential to cultivate healthy relationships through growth and nurture, even if healthy relationships entail experiencing pain. As the age-old saying aptly states: "No pain, no gain." Ultimately, it's crucial to accept that facing rejection from someone is less agonizing than remaining trapped in a self-imposed prison of isolation and loneliness. Each new rejection challenge demands the construction of a fresh wall of self-protection, perpetuating this cycle. Upholding these new defenses is a constant task that requires time, effort, and energy.

Our self-protective walls create multiple layers of obstacles to overcome. Once we realize that these walls, instead of protecting us, actually imprison us, we can start emerging from self-isolation. Our emergence is akin to peeling layers off an onion. It demands time and effort, rendering it a complex process. The more we've maintained these walls over time, the more extended breaking free will be. Therefore, our journey toward freedom is not a single action but necessitates a strategic and ongoing action plan. Walls built and upheld for an extended period may require more time to dismantle and cease their negative impact on our lives.

BREAKTHROUGH

Once we have grown tired of being in our prisons of self-isolation, we are ready for the breakthroughs needed to change. To start this process successfully, we must:

EMBRACE MEANINGFUL RELATIONSHIPS

We need to cultivate genuine connections with others, whether reconnecting with old friends, strengthening existing bonds, or forging new relationships as a catalyst for personal growth.

CONFRONT AND ACKNOWLEDGE PAIN

Rather than concealing our emotional wounds, we must confront them head-on. This means acknowledging our pain, addressing its source, and actively working through it. We can only heal and truly move forward by acknowledging our vulnerabilities.

DISMANTLE THE WALLS

Self-isolation often leads to the construction of emotional walls and defenses. To unlock our full potential, we must dismantle these walls that keep us from fully engaging with others. By letting go of these self-imposed restrictions, we liberate ourselves to become more productive, creative, and open to life's opportunities.

Once I recognized what was happening and how my walls of self-protection were hurting me, I knew I had to make some positive changes. This led me to reach out to the people I had tried to hide from behind my walls of self-protection. Instead of going into the flight response, I went into a positive mode of responding positively to them instead of negatively. Like me, it's essential to acknowledge how we've isolated ourselves due to our self-imposed limitations. We must undergo a fundamental shift in our thinking to initiate a continuous transformation. This change in mindset enables us to recognize how our pain has led us to develop dysfunctional behaviors, much like a neglected child's development.

As long as we remain dysfunctional, our dysfunction will cripple us and those we come into contact with. We must work hard to succeed as adoptive parents need to help their children recover from a lack of care. The longer we take the steps to stay free, the more we will see our negative cycles being broken. We must consciously change our mindset to stop isolating ourselves and breaking negative cycles.

We can reduce feelings of loneliness by proactively changing our behavior and increasing our social connections. When we reach out and connect with others, we shift from feeling like victims to feeling like overcomers. This change in attitude not only benefits us but also encourages others to do the same. Transitioning from victims to overcomers has a positive influence on both ourselves and the people in our lives. We strive to build healthy relationships, even with people we may have avoided, which fosters a positive and supportive environment.

A positive attitude towards our rejection challenges creates a motivating atmosphere for others to follow. Our attitude change profoundly affects our relationships. Therefore, instead of hurting, pushing away, or rejecting others, we build them up by celebrating and encouraging them by opening their eyes to see how their walls affect them and others. Realizing that we cannot protect ourselves completely, no matter how hard we try, can be a liberating and transformative insight. This realization can lead to several positive developments in our lives.

Understand that it's impossible to control every aspect of our lives and shield ourselves from all harm by trying to alleviate the constant stress and anxiety associated with trying to do so. It lets us let go of the burden of always being on guard. Instead of investing time and effort in building and maintaining emotional or metaphorical walls for self-protection, we can direct our energy toward what truly matters. This can include personal growth, pursuing our passions, and building meaningful relationships.

Accepting our vulnerability can help us develop emotional resilience. We learn to adapt to challenges and setbacks rather than resist or deny them, which are critical to personal growth and well-being.

By confronting our pain instead of hiding from it, we experience inner peace and freedom. Our lack of self-protective walls frees us from our negative feelings of isolation and being trapped victims. By letting go of our negative emotions and victim mentality, we develop a positive attitude and outlook on life, seeing things as we should. We consciously turn our lemons into lemonade and see our life glass as half-full instead of half-empty. We then learn how to view our lives accurately and understand that avoiding pain only leads to more pain. It's not a one-time event to break this negative cycle. We must continue to work on our rejection challenges as they take time and effort to break.

INSPIRE

Releasing our self-protective walls has a positive influence on our future relationships. Cultivating healthy relationships is vital to prevent self-imposed isolation from our fear of rejection. We inspire others to take chances through our vulnerability, conquer our hurdles, and show that self-protective walls do more harm than good. Illustrating three key points:

DEVELOPING MEANINGFUL RELATIONSHIPS

Meaningful relationships are a cornerstone of a fulfilling life. They offer a profound source of joy, support, and connection and affect our well-being and happiness. Nurturing and maintaining these relationships are essential for personal growth and contentment.

CONSTRUCTIVE CONFRONTATION OF PAIN

Rather than striving to appear invulnerable, confronting our emotional pain is more constructive. Acknowledging and addressing our pain can lead to personal growth, resilience, and healthier emotional well-being. This shift in approach is vital for our overall development.

DISMANTLING UNNECESSARY BARRIERS

Releasing the burden of maintaining self-protective walls can significantly boost our productivity. Instead of investing time and energy in upholding these barriers, channeling our resources toward more productive endeavors can lead to personal and professional growth, ultimately enriching our lives.

We inspire others to avoid isolation and form healthy relationships. The encouragement and help gained from their healthy relationships help them see how they are part of a bigger team to help them be most effective. When they choose to no longer work as lone rangers, it enables them to receive what others have to give them.

Working effectively with others can help them recognize how valuable it is to work together to help each other in need. As they allow themselves to work with others, they see the benefit of celebrating each other instead of tolerating each other. The more they practically learn to work together as a united team coming alongside each other, the more strength they feel.

With their increased strength, they become more effective in their tasks. Others inspire them to keep going by recognizing their contributions to the team and the importance of building strong bonds. This enhanced awareness of their value and the effectiveness of their peers boost their overall efficiency. As others assist them, they express gratitude and celebrate their value to the team and shared goals. They can foster honor and respect by celebrating others instead of excluding or tolerating them. Being respectful towards others enhances the quality of their environment.

Leaving our self-isolation can positively inspire others that face the same challenge. They see the joy exhibited and are inspired to want the same freedom. Their freedom starts by opening their eyes to see the walls they must deal with and have torn down. They make the same choices as others by seeing how freeing it is when they allow their walls to be torn down. Seeing others' freedom inspires them to keep breaking down their self-protective walls, even though it takes a lot of work.

As they allow their walls to be torn down, they experience freedom and a newfound energy, becoming most effective at what they do. Inspiring others to see their value and worth helps them value and honor the worth of the ones surrounding and helping them. Improving their effectiveness changes their negative opinions when they can help others. This leads to increased trust with those they previously feared.

Being inspired to confront their fears can enhance their relationships with others. When they face their fears, they can inspire others to address their pain instead of shielding themselves behind emotional walls. This motivates them to seek a similar liberating transformation in their lives. Through our example, we show that prolonged isolation can exacerbate and prolong their pain and discomfort.

However, we inspire them to experience ongoing transformational freedom and release as they release their pain. Finally, as they break through their pain instead of running from it, they inspire others to do the same. Others see the change, joy, and peace they can enjoy as they with their self-protective walls of imprisonment. They inspire others to embrace those around them instead of rejecting them. By breaking through their walls, they understand the anguish of rejection. They aim to make others feel supported and valued as they overcome loneliness and isolation.

CONCLUSION

It does not matter how hard we try to build and maintain our walls of self-protection; others who know our weak spots of vulnerability can still penetrate our walls. Let's allow our healthy relationships with others to be our protection instead of our walls of self-protection. We all continually have to face rejection challenges, but with the right people around us, we can master them together.

I transitioned from a state of loneliness and daily dread to a place of hope, joy, and excitement for what lies ahead. Instead of my weekends being a source of despair and discouragement, I anticipated them with happiness. After conquering a distinctive and formidable challenge, I discovered the pleasure of building solid connections with others. By prioritizing relationships over barriers, my life took a positive turn.

APPLICATION

1. Can you recognize the walls you built because of the rejection challenges you've faced?

2. Are you willing to go from depressing loneliness to a place of freedom and joy?

3. Are you able to see why people isolate themselves from you instead of working together with you?

4. What steps are you willing to take to escape your prisons of self-isolation and loneliness?

5. What steps will you take to help others escape their prisons of self-isolation and loneliness

CHAPTER TWO

THE CHALLENGE

OF THE FEAR OF MAN

As I sat in my geography class, filled with much activity, Mr. Jones once again dictated notes for our lesson. My thoughts were different from what he was trying to teach us. I counted the time to recess to go to the custodian's tiny office. Because his daughter was disabled, she could not walk or talk. He was kind to me because he could relate to my cerebral palsy challenges. His office became a haven for me, protecting me from the teasing of my classmates who often asked, 'Why do you speak differently? Why do you move differently?' They enjoyed my occasional awkward movements when they knocked sandwiches from my hand. After school, they would sometimes take my backpack and have me retrieve it to make fun of my slower pace, all while laughing at me.

BREAKDOWN

Rejection challenges can make us afraid of others becoming stuck in a negative cycle. This fear has three outcomes.

IT AFFECTS OUR CONFIDENCE AND BOLDNESS

The fear of being our true selves can severely impact our self-confidence and diminish our ability to act boldly. This fear of self-expression often leads to self-doubt and inhibits personal growth and authenticity.

CAUSING FEAR OF AUTHORITY FIGURES

Our fear of those in positions of authority results in an unhealthy level of defensiveness and heightened sensitivity to their words and actions. This fear can hinder effective communication and collaboration, negatively affecting our relationships.

MAKES US FRUSTRATED, AND ANGRY

When driven by fear, we may exhibit needy, unapproachable, frustrated, and angry behaviors toward others. These reactions stem from a lack of emotional balance and the inability to manage our fears effectively, ultimately hindering our interactions and overall well-being.

Facing fearing how others will respond or react can lead to a constant need to please everyone and being gripped by the fear of rejection or adverse reactions. This can cause us to lose sight of our true selves and erode our self-confidence. I will delve further into self-confidence in a later chapter. Our fears can push us to become people-pleasers, constantly adapting to our surroundings like chameleons. This perpetual quest to please others prevents us from being confident in our skin, leading to self-doubt and indecision. Our wavering mindset obstructs our focus on our identity and what we offer. Instead of setting boundaries out of fear, we put on a façade, hoping it will be enough to keep others from pushing us away. We may think, "If I can't keep others away from me, then I'll make them happy."

One of the most incredible things that caused me to fear people, especially children or those in authority, was their words. Those in authority in my family, school, and peers negatively affected my life through their negative words. Their negative words, knowingly or unknowingly, caused me to be hypersensitive to their words or actions toward me. Having been hurt by the words of those in authority, I found it hard to value and respect those in authority as I should. Therefore, I battled to obey and submit to them, not loving the importance of being willing to be accountable. My hurt caused me not to place a value on what they offered, resulting in my dishonoring and not trusting them. My response to those in authority changed after I realized the value of honor, trust and submission to those in authority.

Unfortunately, the fragmentation of the family structure has caused deep wounds for many young individuals. Even when their fathers are present, they don't want them to have any authority over them. However, we all have to be under some authority in this world. I can't expect others to submit to me if I cannot submit to someone else. When I obey and submit to those in authority, I set a good example for others to follow. Authority figures should earn respect rather than forcing others to submit. We should show it to others through our submission to someone.

Saying: "You would not hear me speak to others in a rebellious way." Instead of: "Don't you ever speak to me that way, I'm in authority over you." People in authority should lead by example, showing their backs to those they lead and showing them where to go next. If we face those we lead, we drive them, causing them to reject us. Authority has been so misused today that many fear those in authority instead of honoring and respecting them. Authority figures can make us feel oppressed and reactive.

When we face the challenge of fear of man caused by those in authority, it makes us unapproachable and unteachable. Fear of others' opinions can lead to a performance-driven mindset instead of a purpose-led mindset. I will take an entire section to talk about being performance-driven later. We get upset when we try to please others and don't get the expected response. However, others are not the problem; we are. As we allow our rejection challenges to drive us, we try to control how we think others should respond to us - forcing them to react in specific ways by dominating, intimidating, or manipulating them. There are better ways to do it than trying to control others. Controlling others through domination, intimidation, manipulation, or seduction can hinder their progress and vision. Therefore, we remember we cannot control others' actions or reactions, no matter how hard we try. We should set an example for others to follow without controlling their response.

BREAKTHROUGH

We break through our fear of man by becoming tired of being fear-driven.

EMBRACING SELF-CONFIDENCE

It is crucial to work on fostering self-confidence to break free from the fear of our authentic selves. Doing so empowers us to embrace our true nature, cultivating a sense of boldness and assurance in our actions.

OVERCOMING FEAR OF AUTHORITY FIGURES

Avoiding excessive defensiveness and heightened sensitivity is essential as we confront the fear of authority figures. Instead, we can learn to value, honor, and trust those in positions of authority, striking a balance that allows for open communication and collaboration. Overcoming this fear enables us to build positive relationships.

MOVING FROM FEAR TO INNER PEACE

The journey from fear-induced behaviors to inner peace involves cultivating a more approachable demeanor and understanding others deeper. By addressing and managing our fears effectively, we can reduce the tendency to become needy, unapproachable, frustrated, and angry. This shift towards inner peace enhances our overall well-being and facilitates healthier interactions with those around us.

As we break through our fear of man's challenge, we experience a newfound boldness in being able to be ourselves, not having to please others. Our courage to be ourselves frees us from being overly needy and trying to get our value and worth from what we do for others. Being released from our fear frees us to know who we are and what we are doing, allowing us to use our capabilities and talents to help others correctly. We no longer use our abilities to get others to accept and approve of us or how we want them to act.

No longer deriving our sense of self-worth from conforming to others' expectations enables us to cultivate greater self-assurance in our true essence and unique contributions to the world. By constantly relinquishing the need to adapt like chameleons, we can dedicate ourselves to our purpose without being torn in different directions. We find contentment in embracing our authentic selves rather than attempting to satisfy everyone by wearing various masks.

We focus on helping others become stronger, not forcing them to please us. As we focus on helping others, we lay aside our fear of being rejected for not offering what we have to give us. We must focus on what we can provide, recognizing that not everyone will accept our offer. Our confidence in what we have to give is so strong that we believe any rejection will be a loss for others, not ourselves. Regardless of how hard we try, we firmly believe that pleasing everyone is an unattainable goal, as others have opinions and decisions.

We often form our opinions out of our hurts from the rejection challenges or hurts we have experienced. We cannot control how others will respond to us. However, we need to choose not to stop trying to help them. When people can be themselves without fear, they feel peaceful and relieved and continue to work towards finding a solution. We are only to work on ensuring our motives, actions, and reactions are pure as we give what we have with all our heart and soul to others.

As a child, I often said: "Sticks and stones may break my bones, but words will never harm me." Life has taught me the exact opposite. Words harm us and often leave long-lasting scars, as their effects are far more invisible than our visible hurts or wounds. Words were the greatest weapon to instill fear and rejection in me. Therefore, my most significant breakthrough came when I recognized the power of people and my own words. Recognizing the power of others' words and my own made me more sensitive to what I would say to others. Knowing my words carried a weighty influence for good or harm. Recognizing the impact of words on myself, I began being more aware of the words I was saying to myself.

Realizing how I spoke to myself during a real-life experience in Israel was a wake-up call. It happened when I was assisting a couple, and in the morning rush, I accidentally dropped an egg from the refrigerator. Instantly, I launched into a tirade of self-criticism, employing my usual negative words. I didn't consider what I was doing, as it had become second nature.

However, the man I was helping overheard my self-deprecating comments and confronted me. He asked me to reflect on the way I was speaking about myself. His reaction opened my eyes to the fact that I had become so accustomed to negative self-talk that I was oblivious to it. I had fallen into a harmful pattern without even realizing it.

This experience reminded us we sometimes need compassionate individuals to guide us in breaking free from our self-sabotaging words and thoughts. In my case, I had become so entrenched in this self-criticism that it had become automatic. It's a testament to the power of support and self-awareness in helping people overcome negative self-talk and ultimately promoting self-growth and self-compassion.

I was so used to speaking negative words about myself that I did not even think about what I was saying negatively about myself. I would be negative about myself before others could because of the negative words I received from peers, teachers, and authority figures. This complex challenge can quickly become a pattern for us as we face rejection challenges that we have to overcome. Gaining an ongoing victory over this unique challenge often takes time and discipline for us to see the breakthrough needed. Many view themselves based on their struggles, thinking they are not attractive, valuable, or successful enough—we breakthrough when we can confidently say good things about ourselves in front of a full-length mirror.

Amanda Hunt's great story "Anger, the Boy, and the Fence" illustrates the power of our words.

"There once was a little boy who had a terrible temper. His father handed him a bag of nails and said he had to hammer a nail into the fence every time the boy lost his temper.

On the first day, the boy hammered 37 nails into that fence. The boy gradually controlled his temper over the next few weeks, and the number of nails he was hammering into the fence slowly decreased. He discovered it was easier to control his temper than to hammer those nails into the fence. Finally, the day came when the boy didn't lose his temper at all. He told his father the news, and the father suggested the boy should now pull out a nail daily. He kept his temper under control.

The days passed, and the young boy could finally tell his father that all the nails were gone. The father took his son and led him to the fence. 'You have done well, my son, but look at the holes in the fence. The fence will never be the same. When you say things angrily, you leave a scar like this one. You can put a knife in a man and draw it out. It won't matter how many times you say I'm sorry; the wound is still there.'"[4]

I learned to overcome my fear of authority by valuing and respecting them. People struggling with the challenge of the fear of man need to change their attitudes and words toward those in authority. They recognize how those in authority, especially fathers who have abused or misused their positions, have hurt them most. However, our hurts do not give us the right to dishonor, undervalue, or disrespect others. If fathers or authority figures reject us, we may act rebellious and struggle to follow authority. We rebel, as our fathers or others have not shown us the correct pattern.

Despite past negative experiences, respecting authority figures can be valuable in helping individuals overcome their fear of authority. Forgiving those who may have caused harm in the past and maintaining a positive outlook can significantly enhance their interactions with others. It's crucial to avoid dwelling on past grievances and instead set a positive example for others in how we view and interact with authority figures.

---

[4] Hunt, A. (2022, January 19). *Anger, The Boy and the Fence*. Alpha Home. https://www.alphahome.org/anger-the-boy-and-the-fence/

One fundamental principle is to submit to authority figures accountable to a higher authority. This creates a system of checks and balances, ensuring we can address any concerns or issues with the authorities to whom they are accountable. By doing so, we can establish trust and break down defensive barriers, fostering more open and productive relationships with those in positions of authority.

Our trust in authority figures should be based on their ability to lead us with respect and consideration rather than forcing submission. Allowing them to show their leadership through their actions can go a long way in building a positive and cooperative relationship. Ultimately, by modeling respectful and accountable behavior to authority, we can inspire others to follow our lead and promote healthier interactions between individuals and those in positions of authority.

My breakthrough over the fear of man freed me and changed my life radically. She showed me how to look at others in non-needy ways, correctly honoring those in authority. My freedom allowed me to serve others without being driven by impure motives. Enabling me to stop, wait, and listen when I felt I was being driven instead of being led before being driven to do what I was not to do. Learning to wait taught me to talk through my feelings with those trying to drive me instead of reacting angrily. The more I did so, the more of a breakthrough I gained and the more teachable I became. I learned valuable lessons through my breakthroughs that I could use to help others.

Those challenged by fear of man must stop, wait, and listen before doing something they're not meant to do. By allowing themselves to be led, they feel peaceful rather than frustrated. Staying peaceful and not getting too frustrated means they don't get angry and leave offended. Leading by example means not controlling others through domination, intimidation, manipulation, or seduction. We need to know our fear-driven triggers and how to respond to them. Our breakthrough over the fear of man causes us to discern clearly when others are controlling us. Being discerning helps us respond peacefully, which creates a positive environment.

INSPIRE

As we make a breakthrough in conquering our fear-driven tendencies, we transform ourselves and become a source of inspiration for others.

EMPHASIZING SELF-CONFIDENCE

This perspective demonstrates the value of being confident in our own identity and having the capacity to give to others. It highlights the power of self-assuredness and generosity in nurturing positive relationships.

PRIORITIZING HONOR AND TRUST

Placing significance on values, honor, and trust when dealing with authority figures underscores the importance of approaching such relationships without unnecessary defensiveness. This approach can lead to healthier interactions and more effective communication.

IMPROVED RELATIONSHIPS AND INNER PEACE

By showcasing the advantages of being approachable, this perspective reveals how fostering open behavior can contribute to improved relationships and greater inner peace. This approach promotes connection and understanding, enriching personal well-being and the quality of our interactions with others.

Through our breakthrough over the fear of man, we can boldly inspire others to gain new confidence to be themselves. By being more confident, they can focus on their task without doubting themselves. Our passionate, joy-filled zeal for what we are doing becomes contagious—and inspires others to develop an attitude of celebrating others and their achievements. Showing them the value of not seeking approval from others prevents them from being chameleons who wear masks to please others. Inspiring others to know who they are and what they are to give to others through their unique capabilities and talents. We inspire others to be led by example by remaining focused and clear on their purpose.

Inspiring others to value and rightly appreciate the power of their words. Awareness of how words affect people's feelings inspires them to be more mindful of their language. All spoken or written words can be destructive, bringing death or life to others. Understanding the power of words inspires them to be careful about how they say things. This inspires them to deliver their words with the right tone and attitude, bringing life and encouragement to others and continually being mindful of how and when they say things. Saying them in an honoring way inspires others to know how to honor, value, and respect authority, primarily through their words—inspiring them to use the right words and tone. Showing an appreciative attitude and approach towards those in authority can help overcome their fear. Respecting authority figures can serve as an inspiration and have a positive influence on others. It is crucial to inspire them to forgive authority figures who have caused harm instead of harboring grudges. Encouraging others to support leaders who demonstrate humility and practical conflict-resolution abilities.

When confronted with conflicts, it is beneficial to address the issue through open communication rather than feeling coerced. Inspiring, honest conversations foster trust and rekindle hope, which makes it easier for others to follow without experiencing fear, frustration, or anger.

We inspire others not to do things out of a need to be needed, helping them not to get angry or feel rejected if others do not accept them. We inspire others to know how to be led with a purpose instead of fear-driven. Being led enables them to discover fulfillment in their endeavors. This satisfaction inspires them to be more receptive and open to learning. Letting go of their defenses, they experience greater inner peace, becoming less prone to anger and no longer feeling controlled by others.

Our freedom encourages others to lead by example, not by forceful control. We inspire others to call people up to a higher standard instead of breaking them down when they make mistakes. We inspire them to learn from their mistakes by allowing them to become their most excellent teaching tools to help others. These teaching tools help others facing similar rejection challenges.

CONCLUSION

Oh, what a joy to go from running and hiding in the custodian's office to being willing to face my fears and effectively overcome them. I couldn't change my cerebral palsy, but I could change how I responded to being different. This brought relief as it lifted a thousand weights off of me. This prevented me from being a people-pleaser or a chameleon, continually looking for another mask to put on to please the ones I was with. I stopped pretending to be someone I was not and started giving my best effort in everything I did. As I did my best to put my heart and soul into what I was doing, I let people respond as they chose to, without me reacting negatively. I could be myself instead of trying to be what others wanted.

One example was when I was called a spastic and told by my fellow student to write quicker in biology class. Instead of negatively reacting, I continued to do the best I could. When he came and apologized a week later, I could boldly say: "I don't care what you call me. I have recently come to accept who I am. Therefore, I am simply working on how I respond to your negative words and not allowing negative attitudes to grow within me."

THE CHALLENGE OF THE FEAR OF MAN

APPLICATION

1. What are you most fearful of when you come in contact with others?

2. How do your words reflect what is going on within you and what you fear most?

3. How do you try to please others?

4. Why do you try to put on different masks for people you come in contact with?

5. What attitudes do you need to change about yourself and others?

CHAPTER THREE
THE CHALLENGE OF
CODEPENDENCY

"Oh no! Not again. Why am I being controlled by this friend I enjoy being with and my co-workers again? What is wrong with them? Don't they know it's wrong to be so controlling and overpowering?" What can I do to stop this cycle I keep falling into when building a solid relationship with a close friend or working with a co-worker?

Frustration and anger welled within me as I felt controlled by a friend and a co-worker as a series of questions plagued my thoughts. I teetered on the edge of an emotional outburst, and my desperation to escape the recurring cycle of this rejection challenge was palpable. This sense of entrapment was all too familiar, and I recognized it was not the first time I'd experienced this sensation of being controlled by someone close to me. I yearned to end this repetitive pattern and finally overcome it. My determination was unwavering; I was determined to break free from the cycle and conquer it this time.

My first reaction was: "How can I get people to stop controlling me?"

However, digging deeper, I realized the problem was not my friend or co-worker but mine. What was fueling this painful cycle? I wanted freedom from the pain and destruction it was causing. My repeated rejection challenges made me over-dependent on someone open to being my close friend, allowing them to control me. When I began working with someone as a co-worker, I would give myself to them so fully I would allow them to control me. Therefore, the problem was not them; it was me. I had to change, not them. I had to decide to break through this vicious cycle of codependency, first with my friends and then with my co-workers, by not depending on one person and being willing to set clear boundaries when I began working with others.

UNHEALTHY CONTROL INSTEAD OF RESPECT

Codependency in close relationships, whether with a friend or co-worker, results in unhealthy dynamics characterized by control rather than mutual respect. These situations often involve one person trying to control the other, which can erode the foundation of trust and respect that should underpin healthy relationships.

NOT MOTIVATED BY RESPECT

Codependency can manifest as idolatry or the unhealthy worship of another person, driven by misguided motives rather than genuine, loving respect. This can distort the relationship dynamics and lead to an imbalance of power and unrealistic expectations, causing harm in the long run.

THE WRONG SENSE OF SECURITY

Codependency can create a false sense of security built on an unstable foundation. This false sense of security can lead to rejection challenges, emotional hurt, and pain when the codependent relationship gets tested in difficult situations. Addressing codependency and fostering healthier independence is crucial for personal growth and, more vital, more balanced relationships.

BREAKDOWN

THE DESIRE FOR CONNECTION

Repeated experiences of rejection can lead individuals to face personal challenges, often driving them to seek deep connections with others. This desire for friendship or collaboration can be powerful but has potential pitfalls.

BALANCING QUALITY TIME WITH BOUNDARIES

Building solid relationships is essential, but excessive attachment to one person, whether a friend or co-worker, can have negative consequences. While quality time together is valuable, spending all free time with a single individual may harm personal growth and well-being.

CODEPENDENCY IN RELATIONSHIPS

When we set no clear boundaries in a working environment, we subconsciously say to our co-workers, "I'm all yours." Giving our all without boundaries allows us to be controlled and dependent. Codependency issues become significantly pronounced when someone is a best friend, with other connections playing secondary roles. Failing to communicate limits can unintentionally signal to co-workers that one is entirely at their disposal, potentially resulting in control.

When we allow a friend or co-worker to dominate us, we may find them manipulating or intimidating us. It is unhealthy when we idolize or worship our friends or co-workers. We rarely realize how things have changed. It's like the story of a frog being boiled alive in water. But if you place it gently in a pot of tepid water and turn the heat on low, it will float there placidly. As the water gradually heats, the frog will sink into a tranquil stupor, exactly like one of us in a hot bath, and before long, with a smile on its face, it will unresistingly allow itself to be boiled to death. [5]

If our pattern of dependency continues, eventually, we become too dependent on the person or a co-worker, leading to codependency. An unbalanced relationship may result from unthinkingly following a friend or co-worker who provides comfort. If we don't recognize this, it can lead to us being driven instead of led by them. Being driven, we make fewer choices of our own. Eventually, we feel trapped, fearful, and controlled by our friends and co-workers. We find our friend or co-worker not wanting to release us to develop other friendships, even with our own family or other co-workers.

This results in them rejecting or finding fault with other friends or co-workers we try to contact. They maintain control over us by giving us multiple things to do as we are willing. Our friend or co-worker may do this without realizing it because of our willingness to accept or reject challenges, past or present.

Their control causes us to become so fearful we think if we don't remain loyal to them, they may reject us. Initially, we submit, not wanting to be rejected by them, wondering if

<hr />

[5]

https://faculty.washington.edu/rturner1/Sustainability/Bibliography/docs/The_Boiling_Frog.pdf something may be wrong with us. Fear makes us double-minded and conflicted.

Addressing indecisiveness involves managing negative emotions and making difficult choices. Sometimes, when a relationship becomes excessively toxic, it may be necessary to end it. Toxic relationships with friends or co-workers can lead to dependency, impaired judgment, and an unhealthy sense of security. Fear can take hold, preventing us from addressing the control we feel until it becomes too late to resolve the issue. This may cause ending the relationship, resulting in facing unforeseen challenges that we would rather avoid. We may damage valuable relationships, hindering our ability to form new friendships or cultivate positive work relationships.

BREAKTHROUGH

Our breakthrough over this codependency challenge comes as we want to improve our future relationships with friends and co-workers.

REJECTING UNHEALTHY CONTROL

Recognize and acknowledge the detrimental impact of unhealthy control and codependency on our well-being. Understand that seeking comfort through these dynamics is counterproductive to our mental and emotional health.

BUILDING DIVERSE, POSITIVE RELATIONSHIPS

Actively cultivate and nurture various healthy relationships in different aspects of life. Resist the tendency to let one individual or co-worker dominate our social and professional spheres, promoting a more balanced and fulfilling social network.

ACKNOWLEDGING CO-DEPENDENCY

Accept the potential for codependency to lead to additional challenges and hardships. Embrace the awareness that breaking free from codependent patterns is crucial for personal growth and the development of healthier connections.

We overcome codependency by first resisting the control of powerful friends or co-workers. This involves breaking free from allowing friends to dictate our actions and establishing clear boundaries for interactions with co-workers. Letting go of controlling friendships becomes a path to comfort and security, even when the individual is someone close, such as a best friend or co-worker.

We learn to honor and respect our friends and co-workers by identifying when we idolize them while understanding the difference between worshiping, honoring, and respecting them. We break free from their control by establishing clear boundaries with them. Having learned from our experiences, we will no longer accept behavior that is controlling or codependent. We recognize the harm caused by controlling relationships with friends and co-workers. Overcoming control and codependency helps us appreciate and value our friends without being controlled by them.

We choose to make new friends and co-workers, even if they might reject us. No longer being controlled by fear, we decide to make healthy friendships with friends and co-workers to break our cycle of codependency. Cultivating multiple healthy relationships provides freedom rather than relying on one controlling friend. Genuine friends and co-workers support our growth in forming healthy connections with others while controlling individuals who may feel threatened by our expanding social circle.

INSPIRE

Our breakthroughs over codependency challenges inspire others to not depend on one person or give our all to co-workers without boundaries.

AVOID SINGLE-PERSON DOMINANCE

Learn to avoid being dominated by a single person, even if their intentions are misguided or they are unaware of their controlling behavior.

EMPHASIZE POSITIVE RELATIONSHIPS

Highlight the significance of cultivating positive relationships. It is essential to associate with individuals who genuinely respect and value us.

EMBRACE SECURITY AND BOUNDARIES

Foster personal well-being by prioritizing security and setting clear boundaries. Experience peace, joy, and healing by establishing healthy limits in various aspects of life.

Breaking through our codependency challenges inspires others to avoid being controlled by a friend. Our courage inspires and liberates others. Gaining the ability to identify codependency within friendships.

We inspire our co-workers to distinguish between being guided and driven and to recognize moments when their friends push them forward, asking themselves, "Is my friend allowing me to be myself, or are they trying to control me?" This encourages others to have several resilient friends surrounding them, no longer giving one person control. This motivates them to build friendships with friends and co-workers on trust and honor instead of dependency. Choosing never to allow themselves to become fear-driven by ensuring they are purpose-led.

Building several strong friendships empowers them and also frees them from codependency. They free themselves from fear and control by looking, pausing, realigning, focusing, and proceeding only when they have unmistakably defined their goals. Understanding the distinction between inspiration and intimidation is critical. Their enhanced discernment motivates them to build strong relationships and collaborate with colleagues without fearing rejection. Opting for collaboration with a diverse and supportive network of friends and co-workers enhances everyone's productivity.

We inspire others to have confidence in their abilities by setting an example of self-control and interdependence. This helps others enjoy the same peace and joy they experience working together without being codependent. This encourages others to build stronger relationships, too. Also, letting go of the pain and hurt they experienced from controlling and driving friends and co-workers inspires them to check their intentions and wants. They reflect on how their actions towards friends and co-workers who display controlling and driving behavior caused pain, inspiring them to check their intentions and wants. We inspire others to have healthy friendships that strengthen their purpose. When they stop being controlled by fear and find their purpose, they experience unexpected healing, freedom, and joy. We inspire others to push through their rejection challenges by sharing our journey of breaking through codependency.

CONCLUSION

Wow! It was a relief to know the dynamics of what was going on and why I kept finding myself trapped in this rejection challenge of being codependent on others. It gave me renewed hope to know how to build the right non-controlling friendships with my friends and why I needed to set clear boundaries with my co-workers. Mastering the art of ending controlling relationships has opened up a new world of fulfilling friendships.

I cherish numerous close and intimate friendships, all characterized by mutual support and growth, with no hint of control or pressure. These relationships contribute to my well-being, fostering positive development as we enjoy evolving together.

APPLICATION

1. What kinds of friends surround you, and do they control you?

2. How freely can you set clear boundaries with those you work with?

3. Do you idolize your friends or have a healthy respect for them?

4. Do you find your friends dominating, intimidating, or manipulating you?

5. Do you feel driven or led to do what you need to by your friends or colleagues?

CHAPTER FOUR

THE CHALLENGE OF BOUNDARIES

"No! Not again! What is going on here? Why was I feeling controlled by my co-worker again?" I was both angry with them and angry with myself. What was going on? Did I require assistance or need to alter my actions or responses to others? As I asked myself these questions, I realized that when I started working with a co-worker, I was unwilling to establish clear boundaries between us. I subconsciously thought that if I laid boundaries, they might reject me. Therefore, I surrendered myself to them and their actions without setting boundaries, expressing: "I am yours entirely-control me." As we saw in the previous chapter, this was the most destructive cycle I kept falling into as I began working with new co-workers, which led to codependency. Therefore, we can see that the challenge of boundaries directly relates to the challenge of codependency, and both challenges connect to rejection challenges.

My lack of boundaries came from my struggles with personal rejection and codependency. I battled to say "No" to what others asked me to do, fearing potential rejection, I hesitated to decline. This relates to our second chapter about the "Fear of Man." My inability to say no resulted in me taking on tasks that were too difficult or unsuitable. My lack of boundaries resulted in several adverse reactions.

SELF-INFLICTED ANGER

Frustration with personal actions and decisions leads to self-blame and regret.

FRUSTRATION AND BURNOUT

Energy-draining activities contribute to growing frustration and burnout, resulting in diminished enthusiasm.

BITTERNESS AND RESENTMENT

Transformation of emotions towards assisted individuals from joy and honor to bitterness and resentment, culminating in anger directed at those fostering a codependent relationship.

BREAKDOWN

We continually see healthy boundaries around us, which we naturally honor without thinking about it. Boundaries are around us constantly, yet we rarely recognize them, as they have become a part of our lives and society. The divisions of time, such as hours in a day and night, days in a week, and months in a year, illustrate established boundaries. Similarly, cities, counties, states, and countries define their territories through boundaries, indicating ownership and prescribing the appropriate ways for individuals to honor and respect their identities. When people don't understand why boundaries are necessary, they struggle to set healthy boundaries for three main reasons.

INSECURITY IN BOUNDARY SETTING

The initial challenge involves understanding why there's a sense of inadequacy in establishing clear boundaries.

FEAR OF MISUNDERSTANDING

A second obstacle arises from the apprehension that others may not comprehend the significance of boundaries, leading to their neglect.

DIFFICULTY IN SAYING "NO"

The third struggle involves taking on unnecessary additional responsibilities because one hesitates to say "no" when appropriate.

In the third section of our journey together, we'll discuss five rejection challenges and address the root cause of the boundary issues. Not establishing clear boundaries often stems from a belief that we need to be more deserving to have our boundaries respected. Frequently, we derive our value and worth from our actions rather than our inherent selves, leading to indecisiveness and confusion.

Therefore, we focus too much on performance rather than purpose. Performance is the subject of the next chapter. If we base our worth on our performance, we may lose our individuality, seeing ourselves as less valuable to others. Many young people face this problem of battling with our values and self-worth today. When we don't base our sense of value and worth on the right foundation, such as our fathers, we may feel compelled to seek our identity through inappropriate avenues and methods. The belief that excelling academically or becoming the best in a job or sport will provide the validation we seek can lead us toward a path lacking fulfillment. Regrettably, these pursuits cannot substitute for the essential elements our fathers should have instilled. This emotional void may contribute to detrimental behaviors, such as substance abuse and engaging in risky sexual activities.

Those who lack identity and self-worth may fear setting boundaries for themselves and others, believing that turning down requests will result in rejection. Everyone must learn the art of setting clear boundaries rather than saying, "Yes to everything." When people don't respect our workplace boundaries, they undermine our value and importance. When people neglect or show disrespect for our boundaries, they diminish their significance.

Not respecting boundaries increases the challenge of saying "no." When we take on what is not the right fit for us, we end up exhausted. Our exhaustion and being robbed of energy by doing too many jobs causes us to lose passion for what we should not be doing. When we lack focus and enthusiasm, we give up on tasks before reaching excellence. When people encounter obstacles, they often lose motivation and abandon projects, resulting in disappointment. Failing to achieve what we promised leads to rejection, resulting in low self-esteem. Rejection causes people to give up on their talents instead of nurturing them. However, their enthusiasm grows when they sense honor, value, and respect, giving them a fresh sense of assurance. The more our courage and confidence grow, the more energized and excited we become. Rather than quitting, we discover a desire to pursue it enthusiastically because it brings us immense fulfillment.

Recognizing the difficulties, we understand the importance of taking action. Yet, our passion for what we can accomplish can be a driving force, especially when faced with rejection challenges. Engaging in tasks to appease co-workers, which we shouldn't be doing, can result in a negative attitude, subpar work, or unfinished assignments.

In the codependency chapter, we saw how we can become controlled if we don't set boundaries when needed. Not having any boundaries communicates our willingness to comply unquestioningly with any request made of us. However, it doesn't take long for the overburdened "willing horse" to experience exhaustion, giving rise to various other opposing challenges. If we leave bitterness and resentment unaddressed, they can escalate into anger and frustration, creating a toxic atmosphere with others. Avoiding challenges can lead to deteriorating work relationships, transforming them into toxic ones.

BREAKTHROUGH

Setting boundaries and being able to say no can pose a challenging struggle for individuals. Triumphing over this rejection challenge can pave the way for positive personal growth.

RECOGNIZING OUR SELF-WORTH

Acknowledge our worthiness to establish boundaries. Seek a father figure and mentor who values and exemplifies healthy boundaries.

ESTABLISHMENT OF HEALTHY BOUNDARIES

Boldly set clear, healthy boundaries for others to honor. Take on only what aligns with our responsibilities.

FREEDOM FROM CONTROL

Embrace clear boundaries to break free from control and avoid harboring bitterness, resentment, frustration, and anger. Cultivate a peaceful and non-toxic environment.

Those who have experienced harm from unhealthy boundaries can confidently gain the ability to establish healthy ones. Our desperation positions us to actively seek the right father figure and/or mentor who can affirm our value, worth, and identity. We must ensure our character development is the focus of their work with us. Learning from them, we can understand the importance of balancing rest and work, which helps us to operate better.

We can seek a mentor to help us become better equipped to perform the tasks as our apprentices. A mentor works primarily to help us develop and refine our skills. This teaches us to improve our work and shows us the value of having the correct work ethic and being diligent workers. Fathers should be concerned about their children's character, ability to rest, and endurance to fulfill their purpose. Mentors focus mainly on the productivity and success of their apprentices in their work. Distinguishing fathers' and mentors' roles will aid us in balancing character and excellence, recognizing that we need both fathers and mentors in our lives as they complement each other effectively.

OVERCOMING REJECTION

Triumphing over rejection and challenges boosts self-confidence and helps people set boundaries confidently, which benefits us and others. Defining precise boundaries removes vague areas of what we will or will not do for others, further avoiding confusion. Fathers and mentors help us gain confidence and skills to learn how to do things correctly. Confident people establish boundaries, knowing how much they will give. Guided by our fathers and mentors, we assert our boundaries to others without fearing rejection, feeling confident they will honor and respect our limits.

The sight of our boundaries being honored encourages us to complete our assigned tasks. Feeling better equipped, we perform our assigned work excellently, acting as good stewards. We maintain our standards of excellence by not letting others invade our boundaries. As our confidence and clarity grow, we refuse to let others invade our boundaries and control us, breaking free from their smothering effect.

Breaking through this challenge of boundaries helps us say "No" to unimportant things and focus on what's essential. The more we can boldly say "No" as needed, the more we cannot say "Yes" to the best things to do. When we express our boundaries, others know what they can and can't do. If someone crosses our boundary, we remind them of our commitment without fear of rejection. When others honor and respect our boundaries, we can both perform better. Their honor and respect make us feel fully fulfilled in what we do, discerning our appointed tasks. When we work from a place of fulfillment, we feel renewed and can accomplish more without getting tired. Why do we feel so much stronger and more energized?

As we experience ourselves being energized through doing the work others have equipped us to do, we do it with dedication and enthusiasm. Filled with energy, passion, and focus, we do our work excellently with joy and peace. Celebrating others' excellent work encourages us to keep going, especially during difficult times. As our attitudes change, it creates a joyful, peaceful, positive environment instead of a toxic one. Creating boundaries can create a friendly environment that attracts people—resulting in others being excited about working with us and inspiring us through their enthusiasm. As our confidence and clarity grow, we liberate ourselves from the smothering effect of others who try to control us and push us towards tasks not aligned with our purpose.

INSPIRE

Through our breakthroughs over boundaries, we inspire others by becoming more passionate about our work. For example:

DEMONSTRATING HEALTHY BOUNDARIES

Highlighting the value of setting healthy, firm boundaries and emphasizing self-acceptance motivates us to establish these boundaries.

GUIDANCE FROM FATHERS AND MENTORS

Highlighting the significance of fathers and mentors in maintaining focus and encouraging rest.

POSITIVE OUTCOMES OF BOUNDARY SETTING

Reveals the positive impact of asserting our boundaries, noting the transformation from potential negativity (bitterness, resentment, frustration, and anger) to joy and peace.

Seeing others' healthy boundaries inspires us to recognize their value, bringing out our unique skills. Recognizing our worth empowers us to set healthy boundaries without fearing rejection. The motivation to find a father figure who emphasizes the growth of our character, not just our skills, stems from our pursuit of self-worth. Allowing our father figure to guide us inspires us to understand the balance between rest and work while cultivating a sense of fulfillment and avoiding hyperactive busyness. Fathers show us how to teach others to honor and respect our boundaries without fear of rejection. The idea of finding a mentor who can help us excel at our skills and be highly productive in our endeavors is inspiring.

Our father, mentor, or fathers and mentors will encourage us to define, establish, protect, and value our boundaries enough to require people to honor and respect them. Clarity about our assigned tasks becomes a source of inspiration, driving us to set and maintain our boundaries. We demand that others respect and honor these boundaries, motivating us to pause, wait, listen, and refocus—especially when we feel overwhelmed and exhausted from our endeavors. When we become overburdened and burned out, we respond negatively due to our experiences. Later, we regret what we said or how we negatively reacted. Others inspire us to recognize and honor the power of saying "No."

THE CHALLENGE OF BOUNDARIES

"No is an anointed word. What you say No to in this period of adjustment may determine what heaven says YES to over your life in the next season."

– Lance Wallnau

Our energy and rhythm motivate us to aim at a consistent and tranquil pace in our work. Establishing distinct boundaries fosters a peaceful atmosphere, encouraging others to define their boundaries.

Remaining peaceful and joyful is the key to our productivity. However, we lose peace and happiness when we get irritated and irritable. We'll inspire others to embrace their unique abilities and not worry about the opinions of others. Our newfound self-confidence inspires others not to be squeezed into another person's mold to please them. Inspiring them to say. "That fits you but does not and will not fit me." This prevents us from becoming bitter or resentful, giving them the freedom to be ourselves. We freely defend our clear boundaries without letting our frustration fester until it ends in an angry outburst.

CONCLUSION

My mentors during my first fourteen years as a traveling teacher motivated and prepared me to excel in what I love doing. Their wisdom, counsel, knowledge, and insights were invaluable. Later, a father figure taught me how to set boundaries and rest when I was successful. He taught me to function peacefully instead of being busy and feeling exhausted. One of the first questions he would ask me when I returned from a teaching trip was not, 'How was it, and what did you accomplish?' Instead, he would say, 'How rested are you?' Having the balance of both a mentor and a father has radically impacted my life, who I am, and what I am doing today. Having both kept me balanced.

In their book "Boundaries,[6]" Henry Cloud and John Townsend provided an illustration. The example involved hiring an office manager. On her second day in the office, I gave her many things to do. About ten minutes later, she knocked on my door with a stack of papers in hand. "What can I do for you, Laurie?" I asked. "You have a problem," she told me. "I do? What is it?" I asked, not having the vaguest idea what she was talking about. "You hired me for twenty hours a week, and you have just given me about forty hours of work. Which twenty would you like done?"

Most of us would not do what Laurie did. We overwork ourselves, become bitter, angry, and resentful, and often think about quitting our jobs.

---

[6] *Boundaries books*. (2024, April 29). Boundaries Books. https://www.boundariesbooks.com/

APPLICATION

1. Why do you feel boundaries are so important after this chapter?

2. Can you boldly lay the boundaries you need for yourself?

3. Can you clearly state what boundaries you want others to honor?

4. Do you fear being rejected for setting your boundaries?

5. How do you react when people don't honor your boundaries?

CHAPTER FIVE
THE CHALLENGE OF
PERFORMANCE

As I walked out of my geography test crying, angry, and frustrated, I asked myself, "What has upset me? My cerebral palsy made it hard to keep up with my peers during exams, resulting in incomplete tests and low grades. This inability to perform as I desired made me most frustrated and unhappy. Being frustrated and unhappy was a cycle repeating itself after I left high school and college. I struggled to transcribe cassette tape teachings verbatim like my classmates. When I probed further with specific questions, I realized my frustration was my focus on performance.

Finally, as I embarked on a career in teaching, a subconscious thought lingered: "If I don't consistently teach, others may reject me." It got to where I would bring someone along to continue teaching, even during leisure activities like fishing. My frustration led me into a destructive pattern until I realized it and started breaking free.

We all want to hear "Well done" or "You did an excellent job." But even more significant than "Well done" or "You did an excellent job," we need to hear the words, "I love and accept you, not for what you are doing, but for who you are." These words destroy the challenge of performance, freeing us to be ourselves. Occasionally, assessing our closest friendships is important by asking, "Are they relating to me or to what I am doing?" I grappled with performance and anxiety for 14 years as a teacher until a father figure played a pivotal role in helping me overcome it.

About 80% of my closest friendships were related to what I did, not to me as a friend. I discovered this after someone challenged me to evaluate my friends surrounding me. I needed to overcome being performance-driven for my future marriage twelve years later. I used to travel 80% of the time before getting married. But after marriage, I reduced it to 20% and didn't find it hard as what I did was no longer my focus. Today, twenty percent of my closest friends relate to what I do for us as a teacher, mentor, or father, while eighty percent relate to me as our friend.

BREAKDOWN

SERVING AUTHENTICALLY

Breaking free from a performance-driven mindset empowers individuals to serve with pure motives. They fearlessly express their capabilities and limitations, fostering transparent and genuine connections.

REDISCOVERING IDENTITY

Liberation from uncontrolled busyness allows individuals to uncover their true identity. Beyond the relentless pursuit of productivity, they embrace authenticity, defining themselves by values rather than external achievements.

RESTING WITHOUT BAGGAGE

Liberation from a performance-oriented approach facilitates rest free from bitterness and resentment.

Individuals enjoy moments of relaxation without the weight of negative emotions, nurturing well-being, and healthier relationships.

Performance-driven individuals often find themselves serving with the wrong motives, driven by a need to be needed and seeking acceptance and approval rather than operating in alignment with their capabilities for the benefit of others. This creates a significant challenge, particularly when the individuals need more appreciation or recognition for their efforts. The perception of having little value and worth emerges, prompting a desire to quit or intensify their efforts.

The misguided motives behind their actions result in pain, hopelessness, and an overall sense of emptiness, contributing to an unfulfilled feeling. It becomes crucial to understand that genuine service should be driven by a sincere desire to contribute rather than being compelled by external pressures or the need for validation. Returning to prioritizing others' expectations over personal fulfillment, as discussed earlier in our journey, it is essential to remember that trying to please everyone often leads to a futile endeavor. Like a chameleon, attempting to adapt to everyone's expectations can eventually result in pleasing no one.

Individuals with misguided motives may struggle to respect boundaries and find it challenging to say "No assertively." This difficulty in setting boundaries can lead to a sense of being controlled and burdened by excessive workloads. The inability to decline unwarranted tasks and responsibilities results in shouldering false burdens, fostering negative attitudes toward those they serve. Our obsession with performance creates fake identities based on our accomplishments. Our achievements make it easier for us to fall into the trap of thinking our value and worth will come from what we have achieved. The more successful we become, the more we try to please others instead of doing what we are best at, being fully equipped to do with all our might. The longer we try to please as many as possible, the more we drive ourselves into hyperactive busyness.

When we are hyperactively busy, we need to pay attention to our responsibilities and show more honor to those we serve. Challenged and active, we lose a sense of purpose and joy, becoming robotic in our actions. When people focus on doing instead of being, we don't realize we're functioning incorrectly. Why have we allowed this to happen so quickly? Being driven to become "human doings" instead of "human beings" has become the norm today for so many, causing us to lose passion and zeal as we are too busy to enjoy it or find fulfillment in the work of our hands.

Taking on extra responsibilities can lead to exhaustion and loss of focus, causing us to want to give up. Losing focus and interest happens when we get tired and overwhelmed by what we're doing. Instead of following our purpose, we let others lead us without enthusiasm for the day ahead. If we don't realize this soon enough, we'll get angrier with others driving us. If we let anger fester towards those driving us, we may become bitter and resentful. As the bitterness and resentment grow towards those driving us, it becomes easier for us to quit what we are doing, not wanting to do it again.

Leaving means others miss out on our unique contribution and what we deserve.

BREAKTHROUGH

CLARIFY MOTIVES AND DECISION-MAKING

To break through being performance-driven, we must check our motives by learning to say "No" when needed. This involves recognizing our responsibilities and ensuring our actions align with our true priorities and values.

ENERGIZE THROUGH PEACEFUL FOCUS

Shift the focus from constant performance to gain energy through peace and rest. Celebrate the achievements and positive qualities of those around us instead of fostering bitterness and resentment. This perspective shift helps bring freedom from the draining nature of a performance-driven mindset.

CONFIDENCE AND EMOTIONAL RELEASE

Rather than being solely driven by external measures of success, focus on growing in confidence as human beings. This involves releasing forgiveness and emotional baggage, fostering personal growth, and embracing a more holistic approach to life.

We can conquer this challenge by understanding the importance of serving with the right motive. Checking ourselves and asking, "Why am I doing this?" helps us ensure correct motivation." Following up with the question: "Am I doing what I should do, or am I doing it for acceptance and approval? Or out of a need to feel needed?

Honest answers to these questions will make us desire to do what we are doing with passion, excitement, and joy instead of being driven to do it. We work with love and devotion, driven by our passion for what we do. We feel fulfilled by our accomplishments. Finding fulfillment in what we are doing makes us excited about doing it and being able to show what we have accomplished to others.

The right motivation makes people feel fulfilled and excited about their work and more willing to help their co-workers. Moving from being driven to being led allows us to become single-focused and motivated from within ourselves. Boldly saying "no" helps us master our passions without taking on unnecessary responsibilities. By breaking through this challenge, we can know what others should carry and understand our responsibilities. Taking responsibility for our tasks makes us feel fulfilled and does not burden others.

Embracing the pursuit of our goals liberates us from the relentless need to please everyone, fostering a sense of security rooted in our functional abilities. Liberation from the people-pleasing mentality enables us to discern our identity independently of our professional endeavors, recognizing that our actions do not define who we are, regardless of the magnitude of our achievements. Sustained passion and unwavering focus serve as bulwarks against the allure of distractions, ensuring that we remain attuned to our objectives and immune to the pull of alternative opportunities.

By channeling our enthusiasm into a well-paced approach, we sidestep the trap of hyperactivity, allowing us to dedicate our utmost efforts to the task. By channeling our enthusiasm into a well-paced approach, we ensure we honor those we serve and can dedicate our utmost efforts to the task. The fruits of our labor, marked by the correctness of our pace and a demonstration of honor, speak for themselves.

Rather than inevitably transforming into mere "human doings" operating on autopilot, perpetually tired and joyless, we reclaim our humanity. We feel human again, accomplishing a set purpose with joy and fulfillment of what we have achieved with excellence. We can think and avoid confusion by focusing on our goal rather than pleasing others. When we stop being confused, we can use our skills to serve others passionately and purposefully. Celebrating someone's passion and hard work with compliments like "great job" or "well done" helps us stay energized and focused.

We feel fulfilled and happy when we get equipped to perform at what we are good at. We can avoid carrying the weight of others' burdens by only taking on what is ours. Fearlessly, we decline tasks we're not equipped to handle without worrying about rejection. Free of exhaustion and overload by not carrying others' responsibilities. Releasing unnecessary burdens allows us to focus on our destiny and do our job excellently. Being responsible for tasks that are theirs, we stay committed to our destined job. Doing a great job with a purpose can energize us instead of making us tired and wanting to quit. When we fulfill our goal, we feel less frustrated and angry. We don't let others or the need to feel needed distract us from our unique purpose. Our frustration and anger go, and so does our bitterness or resentment, as we no longer allow others to drive or control us. We experience this freedom from these negative emotions; we can help others to find our unique purpose, too. Discovering our amazing goal teaches individuals to stay in their lane and not burden others. Our collaborative efforts lead to recognition of our accomplishments.

INSPIRE

MOTIVE CHECK AND RESPONSIBILITIES

We prioritize a "Yes or No" approach to check motives and emphasize clear definitions of responsibility. This cultivates transparency and integrity and fosters accountability within our performance-driven culture.

ENERGIZED BY POSITIVE CELEBRATION

Our commitment to being performance-driven includes fostering an energized and focused mindset. This positivity permeates our celebrations, creating an atmosphere that uplifts and inspires continued success.

IDENTITY AND JOYFUL LEADERSHIP

Recognizing an individual identity is critical to growth. We promote self-awareness, encouraging team members to understand their strengths and values. Our leadership is anchored in joy, creating a purpose-driven environment for collective fulfillment and success.

Our breakthroughs over our performance challenges motivate others to see us serve with the right motivation. We inspire others to see how important it is to be focused and passionate about what we are doing and then do it with all our hearts and soul. We must motivate others to honor and serve those we have committed to with our hearts and souls. Serving others helps if we're being led or driven. We inspire those around us to prioritize our work and not feel guilty for saying "No."

Breaking through this challenge inspires others to stop being people-pleasers. Instead of being driven to please everyone, we inspire ourselves to satisfy only the ones we have committed ourselves to. This freedom to be led instead of be driven inspires others to find our security in knowing what we are to function passionately in.

Inspiring others to see our identity in who we are instead of basing our identity on how well we work. As we correctly find our identity, we no longer find our value and worth in what we achieve but in who we are. By finding our identity, in whom we inspire others, not to be sidetracked by doing good things to please everyone. We are passionate and focused on our commitments, achieving excellence without getting sidetracked. Concentrating on one thing helps us do it well and without stress. We respect those who equip us to work uniquely.

Embracing the triumphs that emerge from overcoming challenges is a powerful source of inspiration for those around us. It encourages them to pursue their endeavors with unwavering passion. The realization that transforming into mere "human doings" diminishes our joy and inhibits the fulfillment of our distinct purpose encourages us to pause, reflect, and attune ourselves before forging ahead.

71

Acknowledging our unique goals inspires us and others to take a moment to rest, listen, and wait before succumbing to the relentless drive that often engulfs us. This intentional pause eradicates the inner conflict and confusion that arises from being double-minded. Instead, armed with a clear sense of purpose, we propel ourselves forward in our work with renewed determination.

Understanding our purpose fuels, a passionate engagement, transforming our tasks into a source of pleasure rather than a burdensome obligation. As we revel in our unique calling, we become beacons of inspiration, motivating others to approach their work fervently and joyfully. The simple yet profound expressions of "Well done" and "Thank you" become rituals of celebration, reinforcing the value of our collective efforts. Prioritizing adequate rest becomes a cornerstone of our success, providing the rejuvenation to sustain our momentum. This sustained momentum becomes the driving force that propels us forward until we diligently and excellently complete the tasks we set out to accomplish.

We inspire others to reflect on goals and emotions. This is by breaking through our challenges and inspiring us to pursue joy and passion in our endeavors, be discerning in choosing only important activities, and stay focused on our unique purpose by selecting only what we need to do. We focus on one thing we are good at instead of trying to be good at everything. Once we become experts, we can recognize when others try to make us do something different or conform to other standards.

OVERCOMING REJECTION

Our wise judgment allows us to say no to things that don't match our skills, freeing us from unnecessary burdens. Our boldness encourages others to remain focused by declining tasks that don't suit us. Breaking through our performance challenges enables us to help others identify our burdens. Through our discernment, we can see what makes us tired, weary, overloaded, and driven instead of filling us with passion and joy. We remain undistracted by others and stay focused on what brings us joy.

By staying focused solely on our purpose, we actively embrace responsibility, which allows us to accomplish it. Our energy and motivation will propel us to keep going with joy. Being energized and focused helps us work best. We no longer feel frustrated and angry as we focus correctly and function clearly. By not getting frustrated or angry, we can't control or drive others like we used to. This makes us less bitter or resentful towards others. We inspire ourselves to know our strengths and how to function best by resisting being driven and controlled. Our accomplishments receive praise because we have maintained a focus on our responsibilities.

CONCLUSION

Wow! Learning that my actions are not who I am was a relief. I enjoy doing tasks that I have learned to do. But who I am as a person or a son is Bradley. This understanding freed me from trying to outperform others or being performance-driven to achieve more. Learning to be myself allowed me to enjoy taking time to rest and relax without teaching someone while I was resting and relaxing. My motivation for serving others changed, as I no longer did it for acceptance and approval but because I found joy in teaching. I could pause and ask myself, "Why am I being driven instead of led?" When I felt myself getting carried away with my work. My friends liked me for who I was, not what I could do for us, which made us celebrate each other instead of competing. This challenge was challenging, but mastering it radically changed what I did and why.

APPLICATION

1. Do you feel compelled to perform or guided to function freely in your work?

2. What motivates you to do what you are doing for others?

3. Has bitterness or resentment built up within you about what you have to do?

4. Does what you do for others take energy away from you, or does it give you energy?

5. Do your closest friends enjoy who you are or what you do for them

SECTION TWO
PANIC

CHAPTER SIX
THE CHALLENGE OF
BEING FORCEFUL

"I will not do this!" I yelled out loud. These words came out of my mouth at two a.m. and startled me. I struggled to complete the assignment of transcribing teachings verbatim from the cassette tapes we provided. I considered what was causing this intense internal storm. Why was I being so forcefully rebellious against what my leaders had asked me to do, as I had not seen myself as rebellious but as a passively compliant type? As I considered what was happening, I recognized a pattern I had not seen clearly until then. When I could not do something and those around me because of my cerebral palsy, I would become frustrated instead of being open and honest with people about it. Eventually, I internally said, "I give up!" in the most rebellious way.

BREAKDOWN

Because of my cerebral palsy, I found it hard to write as fast as my classmates, which made me feel frustrated and respond negatively. I reacted negatively by being forceful towards those who didn't understand. My open forcefulness stemmed from my frustration that it took me so much longer than my fellow students to complete my writing assignments. This issue frustrated me for years, and I had to stop being overly forceful about moving forward and relate better to others.

NEGATIVE IMPACT OF FORCEFUL BEHAVIOR

When individuals are excessively forceful, it becomes clear and easily detectable by those nearby. An uncharming and unreserved expression of feelings characterizes this forcefulness, leaving no room for subtlety. Such individuals often exert control through vocal dominance, overpowering others. The forceful behavior may stem from rejection, leading to the use of negative words to assert control over others.

LONELINESS AS A CONSEQUENCE

One significant consequence of forceful behavior is the isolation it breeds. Forceful individuals risk pushing people away, as their dominating demeanor creates an emotional distance. The inability to form authentic relationships because of overpowering tendencies contributes to a sense of loneliness. Frustration and anger compound this loneliness from the struggle to conform to societal expectations and fit into predetermined molds.

CHALLENGES FACED BY YOUNG PEOPLE

In contemporary society, some young individuals struggle to express themselves assertively. Pursuing fulfillment often leads them to explore avenues such as engaging in sports or striving for academic achievements. While these endeavors may offer temporary satisfaction, they frequently fall short of filling the underlying void. Challenging authority and ignoring the perspectives of others can harm relationships and disrupt the harmony of the workplace. In times of rejection, some individuals seek negative attention through aggressive actions or words, exacerbating their challenges and those around them.

The insights derived from military research conducted by a team of psychologists and sociologists involving a sample of 200 children aged 3 to 18, whose fathers were absent due to military service, reveal notable correlations between the absence of a parent and various psychological outcomes:[7]

Rage – Crime:

o   The study suggests a link between the absence of a father due to military service and the manifestation of rage in children, potentially leading to criminal behaviors. The lack of a parental figure appears to be associated with heightened emotional responses.

Denial and Fantasy – Personality Disorders:

o   Children experiencing the absence of a military-serving father may cope through denial and immersion in fantasy worlds. This coping mechanism is indicative of potential connections to the development of personality disorders, highlighting the impact of prolonged parental absence on psychological well-being.

---

[7] Thompson, B. R. T., & Thompson, B. R. (1989). *Walls of my heart.*

Reunion Attempts – Possessiveness:

○   The research indicates that children in such circumstances may make persistent attempts to seek reunions, a behavior associated with possessiveness. This suggests that the absence of a father can contribute to an intensified desire for connection and possession.

Guilt – Depression Internalized – Delinquency Externalized:

○   The absence of a father figure is linked to feelings of guilt, with internalized guilt potentially leading to depression. Conversely, externalized guilt may manifest in delinquent behaviors. This underscores the complex emotional consequences associated with parental absence.

Fear – Neuroses:

○   The research identifies a correlation between the absence of a military-serving father and the emergence of fear, potentially indicative of neuroses. The heightened fear responses in children point to the psychological challenges they face in the absence of a parental presence.

Impulse Changes – Psychosomatic Disorders:

○   Children experiencing the absence of a father may exhibit changes in impulses, suggesting a potential connection to the development of psychosomatic disorders. The disruption in emotional stability may manifest physically, impacting overall well-being.

Régression – Psychoses:

o   The study reveals that in the absence of a father due to military service, children may experience regression, reverting to earlier developmental stages. This regressive behavior is associated with psychoses, highlighting the profound impact of parental absence on mental health outcomes in children.

Rejected people may become forceful, making it difficult for others to reach out and build genuine friendships with us. Being too aggressive because of fear of rejection can harm relationships with co-workers and friends by breaking trust and respect. People who become too forceful may not share their feelings because they're frustrated.

We get mad because we feel isolated and alone. We feel alone and isolated because we don't know why we fear being too forceful with our friends or colleagues. When feeling isolated, people experience similar emotions to those dealt with in the first challenge of walls. In our first chapter, I discussed this when we spoke of individuals who built walls around themselves, thinking it would protect them.

When rejected, people become pushy and avoid being honest about their struggles, showing us the importance of admitting our difficulties and humility. Not being honest makes us wait too long to respond. We end up frustrated and give up. Rather than seeking help or talking to someone, we give up easily. When forced into an unsuitable mold, we react the same way with friends and co-workers. Saying, "I will not do this." Trying to fit into the wrong mold can make people feel sad and stuck, and our fears can make us stay there longer than we should. The longer we remain trapped, the harder it becomes for us to recognize what is happening. If we don't deal with our feelings correctly, it can rob us of our joy and prevent us from fulfilling our unique life purpose, making us feel smothered instead of mothered and trapped instead of free to express ourselves. People who lose happiness and purpose may become angry and forceful rather than discussing their feelings with others. We understand that fitting into a mold not designed for us causes frustration and may lead us to respond by being overly forceful.

BREAKTHROUGH

RECOGNIZING RESPONSES

To overcome the challenge of being overly forceful in our reactions, the first crucial step is acknowledging the origin of this behavior. It requires introspection and self-awareness to understand the root causes that trigger forcefulness. By being mindful of our words, actions, and reactions, we can cultivate a heightened awareness of how our behavior impacts ourselves and those around us. This self-awareness lays the foundation for transformative change.

STOP PUSHING PEOPLE AWAY

A significant aspect of addressing forceful tendencies involves breaking the habit of pushing people away.

Instead of maintaining a distance through overpowering behavior, we must actively work towards reaching out and fostering connections. This shift requires consciously building bridges and engaging in open communication. By embracing inclusivity and connection, we can replace isolation with meaningful relationships and collaboration.

HONESTY WITHOUT COMPROMISING

The third key element in this transformative journey is honesty about the molds we have constructed for ourselves. It involves candidly evaluating the expectations and societal norms that may have influenced our behavior. While acknowledging these molds, we must be honest about our authentic selves and resist compromising our true identity. Balancing societal expectations and personal authenticity allows genuine growth without succumbing to external pressures.

This challenge of being overly forceful is the easiest for others to identify and know what is going on. We struggle to recognize our usefulness because of issues with others. Being open and honest with ourselves is essential to achieving the breakthroughs. Once we remove what has been blinding us, we should ask trusted ones to help identify our blind spots. It takes time to recognize the need for help and ask for it. People should be patient with themselves and not rush. Listening to our words can help us realize internal battles that affect our behavior towards others. Our words reflect our inner state and help us recognize what we need to address and how it affects our interactions with others. How we talk about ourselves affects how we speak to others. Being aware of the impact of our words, people should be careful and considerate of what we say. It can help us notice problems before we become too aggressive.

We need to reconnect after rejection. In addition, reach out to others, accept their help, avoid rejecting them, and choose not to leave or reject others because they can't provide what we need. Strong and healthy relationships are better than superficial ones based on personal needs or wants. Positive relationships with others can reduce the confusion and pain of rejection. We must create harmony instead of conflict to prevent a hostile work environment. A positive work environment helps people feel less afraid of others. Overcoming fears helps us be less forceful and more relational with others.

Individuals who experience rejection often articulate their thoughts with boldness yet without negativity, especially when faced with an inability to complete a task. Demonstrating courage, we assertively decline when our peers push us beyond our capabilities. To mitigate the escalation of internal conflicts, individuals must voice their concerns and seek help from others to address issues calmly. This approach encourages honest acknowledgment of our weaknesses instead of persevering with unwarranted pride.

For those grappling with rejection, expressing frustration promptly and composedly is essential. Communicating one's feelings regarding the tasks or molds imposed upon us is imperative. Each of us is akin to a unique set of fingerprints, and despite the appearance of compatibility, there are more fitting paths for us. Embracing our individuality becomes paramount. To live a life devoid of comparisons or regrets stemming from the attempt to fit into others' molds, we must recognize and value our differences. An illustrative anecdote is a poignant reminder: a parent once told his son, "You will be like that person." The son astutely replied, "I am most disappointed, as I wanted to be a first me, not someone else." This narrative is a powerful affirmation to cherish our uniqueness rather than aspiring to be someone else or conforming to molds not meant for us.

INSPIRE

CHOOSING POSITIVE BREAKTHROUGHS

By choosing positive breakthroughs over being forceful, we inspire others to recognize the importance of seeking what we need with mindfulness in our expressions and actions.

BUILDING CONNECTION

Through our example, we can guide people to break the habit of pushing others away and encourage them to reach out, fostering a sense of connection and collaboration.

EMPHASIZING HONESTY AND INDIVIDUALITY

Our approach underscores the significance of honesty about the molds imposed upon us without compromising our individuality. This emphasis promotes a culture of authenticity and self-acceptance.

We can inspire people to explore the root of their forceful instincts by teaching them self-worth and encouraging them to consult with people they trust and respect. Seeking insights from those they trust can help them understand the underlying causes of our forceful behavior. We inspire them to value honest advice and insights, contributing to their effectiveness in word and deed. Inspiring them to focus on their internal and external words and reflect on their thoughts. Whether directed at themselves or others, their words are crucial in determining whether we respond positively or negatively. Instead of using words to control or overpower, they should use them calmly to build themselves and others up.

We inspire them to connect with those around them and promote their well-being and peace. Inspiring those in controlling relationships to reach out to others instead of resisting can inspire us to keep going. Helping them understand the importance of establishing new relationships grounded in honor, trust, and respect. By attempting to do this, we will reap the benefits of not feeling alone and having friends and strong relationships surrounding us. Fear stops rebellion in relationships and creates a positive environment.

It's possible to inspire people to overcome their fear of the actions and reactions of others, even when we resist being forced into the wrong molds. We inspire them to express themselves calmly when they cannot complete a task or feel overwhelmed. By inspiring them to do this, we can help prevent them from feeling frustrated and angry. We can inspire them to be self-assured and not feel the need to compete with others. We are inspiring them to embrace their individuality and feel appreciated.

CONCLUSION

Being forceful is a big issue for young people today. If we can overcome it, our lives will be happier and more peaceful, which will benefit us too. Several years ago, I attended a seminar where a doctor would talk about the problems of sexually transmitted diseases. She had to deal daily with young people coming to her for help. She said fathers need to acknowledge their teenagers, and that's causing a lot of problems. It surprised me.

A good friend wrote two books on how fathers need a rite of passage ceremony for their sons and daughters when they turn thirteen. This is a friendly approach to preventing several negative issues, including rebellion or being forceful.

For the older generation, forgiving our fathers who did not give us what we needed is necessary. My friend dreamt he was in a hotel room with his family, feeling sad and crying because his father didn't show affection. When his father asked him why he was crying, he told him, and his father responded by reaching his arms out to hug him, but as he did so, his arms disappeared. He was told that his father couldn't provide him with what he never got from his father. He forgave his father and looked for a different father figure who could give him what he needed. This affected his relations with his natural father. We could be closer than ever from then on and became the best of friends until the day his father died.

APPLICATION

1. What causes you to become forceful?

2. To whom can you turn for help when you get frustrated?

3. Why is it important to have people to help you when you become forceful?

4. How has being forceful affected your relationships with friends?

5. Can you be honest enough to tell people when they try squeezing you into their mold?

CHAPTER SEVEN
THE CHALLENGE OF
BEING OVERPOWERING

I had the chance to teach at a famous teacher's board meeting and helped him understand something he hadn't done in 40 years. It was a fantastic event. A US organization invited me to travel and teach during our 25th-anniversary celebration. It allowed me to be on the same stage as a world-renowned teacher. These were the kinds of statements I would make when I got into a new group, trying to impress, hoping it would cause them to accept me instead of rejecting me.

Those who have experienced rejection worry about being rejected by groups that don't know them well and judge them based on first impressions. Therefore, instead of sharing their strengths and building relationships, they rebel against them and become overpowering.

BREAKDOWN

DEPLOYMENT OF GIFTS AND ABILITIES

Rejected individuals often resort to overpowering to gain recognition from those they aspire to collaborate with. They employ their unique gifts and abilities, coupled with influential personalities, to persuade others of their value and capabilities.

OVERPOWERING PRESENCE

A second tactic involves creating an atmosphere where people's vision becomes unclear, as the rejected individuals overpower the collective perspective. This subtle manipulation aims to divert attention away from their rejection and refocus it on their asserted strengths and qualities.

PRIDEFUL AND UNTEACHABLE SPIRIT

In seeking acknowledgment, individuals facing rejection may adopt a prideful and unteachable demeanor, allowing this spirit to govern their actions and reactions. This approach may serve as a defense mechanism, shielding them from the vulnerability of acknowledgment and acceptance.

Insecurity and rejection can lead people to use their talents or personalities to control others. We'll discuss this in Section Three. When we do this, we misuse our gifts and abilities or forceful personalities. We make others feel overpowered, confused, and intimidated by us as we try to impress us in deceptive ways. People who face rejection may influence others negatively instead of respecting our choices. [8]James McNally studied motivation to understand its dynamics. Motivation is a subject that has been greatly misunderstood. Therefore, I did a thesis on this during my post-graduate studies. After extensive research, I concluded: 'That which many people call motivation is not motivation at all; rather, it is positive and negative stimulation.'

---

[8] McNally, J. (2011b). *Sonship: The Word Made Flesh.*

Let me explain: If a dog is lying in a doorway you wish to go through, there are two ways to cause him to move. First, you might offer him a treat; this is an example of 'positive stimulation.' If this does not work, you can kick him; this I would call 'negative stimulation.' I like to call what I have described here The Coaxing or Kicking Model. In the two examples, the dog is stimulated, not motivated. Who wants the dog to move, you or the dog? The dog moves, but you desire the dog to move. Hence, you are the one who is motivated. The dog is simply responding to your stimulus. It is only if and when the dog moves of its desire that the dog is motivated."[9]

Individuals who have experienced rejection may subtly overpower others, employing negative stimulation to sway others, clouding our perception. Our self-admiration can be misleading, as our fear reveals hidden intimidation. Seeking acceptance and approval from external sources can provide a false sense of value and worth rooted in the wrong foundation. Adopting a Lone Ranger mentality, believing we are unparalleled in our abilities, reflects a dangerous lack of character and maturity. Overcoming immaturity and childish behavior is imperative, as failure to do so could ultimately jeopardize our gifts. When misused in this manner, our abilities become disconnected from our character. While our skills and accomplishments may dazzle, our character truly matters, especially when facing intense pressure. Demonstrating good fruit in such moments becomes crucial, as it reveals our genuine character and serves as a magnet,

---

[9] McNally, J. (2011). *Sonship: The Word Made Flesh.*

either attracting or repelling those who wish to collaborate with us.

Embracing this undercurrent of subtle overpowering fosters a prideful attitude, projecting to others that we consider ourselves unmatched in our abilities. We should focus on doing our best work and let others decide if they want to work with us based on our actions, not our words. When we allow a prideful attitude to develop, we become stubborn, defensive, and overly protective about what we can do well.

Our prideful attitude makes us unwilling to expose our weakness to others because they may reject us for doing so. We can learn valuable lessons from our mistakes, like the Jewish people who learn from their past failures to avoid repeating them in the future. Being overpowering and stubborn makes us unteachable and not open to being corrected when we should be. When this attitude continues, we become angry with anyone who tries to correct us or show us our weaknesses, causing us to become controlling.

BREAKTHROUGH

SERVITUDE WITH GENUINE MOTIVATION

Acknowledging the misuse of talents and personalities to control others is a pivotal first step towards positive change. Individuals must journey to serve others with genuine and altruistic motivation to break free from this pattern. This shift marks a transformative process, redirecting their focus from manipulation to authentic contribution.

CRAFTING A PURPOSEFUL VISION

The path to redemption involves a crystal-clear vision of how one's abilities can authentically benefit others. This clarity enables individuals to channel their talents wholeheartedly, offering valuable contributions with sincerity. Leading by example, they underscore the importance of character and the genuine fruits of their labor, becoming beacons of inspiration for others to follow.

EMBRACING TEACHABILITY AND HUMILITY

Individuals must cultivate a spirit of teachability and humility to break free from the chains of misuse. This entails a willingness to acknowledge mistakes and shortcomings, fostering an environment conducive to growth and learning. Embracing humility becomes the bridge to personal evolution, paving the way for healthier interactions and collaborations.

We must change our attitude and lead with a servant's heart instead of using our talent, ability, or personality to convince people to accept us. Our top priority should be to please our mentor and grow, not to please others or seek validation. Through our diligent work ethic, we must impress people through our actions rather than controlling words, which can be deceptive. We must do an excellent job with no manipulative control. We must desire to help be better at what we are doing and impart our expertise to be most effective at what we are doing.

Instead of manipulating or controlling people, we should guide them with a clear vision of our goals and help them achieve them. We should hone our character and strengths during difficult times to better serve others and find fulfillment. We should show our care and service instead of imposing our talents, abilities, and personalities on others and allowing our actions and reactions to speak louder than our words.

We need to see ourselves as part of a team with unique talents and abilities. These are to help and complement others' unique talents and skills as much as we are there to complement ours. It is essential not to allow ourselves to fall into a Lone Ranger mentality, thinking we are the best and no one else can do it as well as we can. Knowing that someone else can replace us if we do not show the right heart attitude to others by submitting to them and being open to letting them teach us so that we will continually learn invaluable lessons from them.

Being receptive to feedback and new ideas benefits us all. Let's recognize our tendency to be defensive and ask others to let us know when we're not receptive to their help. We must humble ourselves and admit our weaknesses when we cannot do something. When we have made a mistake, we need to ask for help, as others have the strength and knowledge to help us. We must realize that we can show new things or more effective ways of doing things if we allow ourselves the opportunity.

INSPIRE

UTILIZATION OF GIFTS AND PERSONALITY

Having experienced a transformative breakthrough, the commitment lies in utilizing talents, abilities, and personality traits for the genuine service and inspiration of others. The focus shifts from self-serving motives to a conscious effort to contribute positively, aligning actions intending to make a meaningful impact.

CLARITY OF VISION AND PURPOSE

Living out the breakthrough involves cultivating a profound understanding of the importance of a clear vision and purpose. Individuals recognize that the true power of their contributions emerges when aligned with a well-defined purpose. This clarity serves as a guiding force, ensuring that their endeavors resonate authentically with the goals they aim to achieve.

EMBRACING HUMILITY AND TEACHABILITY

The continued practice of humility and teachability is central to the breakthroughs. Acknowledging that growth is an ongoing process, individuals remain humble and open to learning from every experience. This mindset sustains personal development and fosters genuine connections and collaborations with those they aspire to serve and inspire.

We inspire others by breaking free from overpowering them and using our talents and abilities. We use our talents and abilities to equip them instead of controlling them. This inspires them to excel and showcase their training. By serving others wholeheartedly, our actions speak louder than our words. We will inspire others to desire what we offer without forcing them to want it and to continually check to see why they are doing what they are doing for themselves or others.

We inspire others to clarify their purpose and vision and guide others to do the same. They realize their actions and qualities can boost others' skills, even when tackling tremendous challenges. Through our example, we inspire them by teaching them how to reach out for help when they recognize bruises and flaws in our character and fruit. Inspiring them to go to the right people to get help before those bruises or blemishes destroy them. We encourage people to see their strengths and values and to work together with others as a united team. We inspire people to be receptive to feedback and constructive criticism. Showing their humility and willingness to be helped and corrected by those they have submitted to work with. We inspire them through our weaknesses and encourage them to seek help when necessary, learning valuable life lessons from others.

CONCLUSION

A flashback echoed, "No, you teach tonight." "But it's your turn to." This was the conversation with a fellow teacher as we traveled and decided on who would teach. Being so peaceful within myself, it did not matter who would teach. As I knew who I was and was secure in what I offered to whoever would receive it. I used to rely on persuasion and being overpowering to seek as many teaching opportunities as possible, but things have changed.

APPLICATION

1. How secure are you about what you have to give others?

2. What convinces people to invite you to join their team or help them?

3. How clear are you about your purpose and vision for what you do?

4. How open are you to learn from others around you?

5. How open are you to let others help you with your weak areas?

CHAPTER EIGHT
THE CHALLENGE OF
BEING DEFIANT

In a poignant flashback, the echoes of a disheartening revelation reverberated: "Stop controlling me!" This marked the second occasion within two years that I found myself confronted with this searing plea from the students under my guidance. Recognizing the urgency to unravel the roots of this recurrent issue, I embarked on a journey to comprehend why this dynamic persisted and, more importantly, how to break free from its cyclical grip. The prospect of continuously navigating this emotional terrain compelled me to delve into the core.

Unlike the previous year, where I opted to disengage when confronted with offenses, I chose a different path this time—I stayed. I was determined to unravel why such reactions surfaced within our interactions. I was resolute in finding and confronting the issue head-on to discern the underlying causes.

BREAKDOWN

COMMUNICATION HINDERED BY FEAR

Individuals may withhold feedback or point out weaknesses in others due to the anxiety surrounding potential judgment or rejection. This fear-driven silence becomes a breeding ground for unresolved issues.

DEFIANT REACTIONS STRAIN BONDS

When confronted with rejection or the perceived threat of criticism, people may respond defiantly, contributing to a breakdown in communication. This defiance intensifies the emotional strain and damages the overall quality of relationships.

PERSONAL FEARS OVER RELATIONSHIPS

The decision to remain silent and avoid addressing concerns reflects a prioritization of personal fears over the well-being of relationships. Individuals might resort to dominating or manipulating others to control reactions, further eroding the foundation of healthy connections.

Fear of rejection can cause some to be silently defiant when in conflict or facing a rejection challenge. We may refrain from talking through our issues with others. Our fears make us interact defiantly with others. We withdraw defiantly and remain silent instead of talking to others. This causes an internal battle. If the internal battle persists, it will lead to a silent bomb that grows stronger and becomes uncontrollable. We explode in anger because we've been keeping too much pressure inside. Not correcting others earlier causes us to regret it. We don't realize that our fear of confrontation causes our angry outbursts, leading us to lash out at others in a harmful way. Acting defiant, dominating, intimidating, or manipulative makes us controlling towards others. Preventing others from making choices can lead to anger and offense. We avoid confrontation and hope others will address the issue before we have to.

Silence can be a response to rejection challenges, even though it's not verbal. We provoked anger from others by staying silent when we should have spoken up. By remaining silent, we upset others who want to know how we truly feel and what we did wrong. Staying silent after rejecting someone can make us angry and more controlling. This upsets others who want to know our true feelings and what we did wrong. This makes others more offended and angrier. Angry friends and co-workers call us out for being controlled. We use silent defiance to control others who want to communicate with us. Instead of speaking up, we stay silent and hope others will notice and question our behavior.

Being silent and withdrawn can destroy relationships and prevent teamwork. Not communicating openly in marriage is a way to control one's partner by making us respond. It often leads to pity when people remain silent instead of discussing challenging issues with their loved ones. This is a topic we will address in Section Three. Silence can ruin friendships and create a toxic work environment. Silent defiance can eventually destroy a marriage if we do not address it in time.

Being silently defiant because of a rejection challenge can ruin friendships, work relationships, and marriages. Rejection challenges can cause people to respond with silent defiance and become aggressive towards others in authority. Those who face rejection may stop correcting or confronting others because of the false belief that it's unacceptable. In the next chapter, we'll learn how rejected people struggle to accept a critique or a tip and may avoid those who try to correct their behavior.

BREAKTHROUGH

IMMEDIATE COMMUNICATION

In response to a pivotal moment with students that jolted my self-awareness, I committed to asking myself challenging questions to prevent recurring mistakes. I recognized that my silent defiance had roots in rejection and detrimentally impacted my relationships with colleagues, so I took a proactive approach. First, I focused on learning to articulate my thoughts promptly to ensure that others could hear me.

ABANDONING SILENT DEFIANCE

Understanding the destructive nature of silent defiance, similar to the silent treatment, I took deliberate steps to eliminate this counterproductive behavior from my interpersonal interactions. Breaking free from the shackles of silent resistance, I sought healthier avenues for expressing disagreements or concerns, fostering open communication and understanding within my professional relationships.

ACCOUNTABILITY AND TRANSPARENCY

To mitigate potential harm caused by my actions, I adopted a mindset of accountability and transparency. This involved acknowledging mistakes promptly and communicating openly when I recognized behavior that could be detrimental to myself or others. By caring enough to address and rectify wrongdoings, I contributed to a culture of honesty and responsibility within my professional sphere.

To overcome this rejection challenge, we should be honest and face the consequences of our actions without being upset. We ask others for permission to correct or point out their areas of need instead of rejecting or controlling them. Once given consent, we should quickly talk to them to avoid internalizing things. We prevent bomb-filled explosions by maintaining our reactions and avoiding overthinking. We stop beating ourselves up for overreacting and fear staying silent. It takes time to learn how to stop overreacting silently. I made things worse by speaking out unnecessarily during my breakthrough period, but I eventually learned to listen first and then respond. It's better to express your feelings than keep them inside and build up pressure. We can learn to speak about our mistakes without getting upset if our friends, co-workers, or spouses allow us to do so.

Don't respond negatively to rejection with silent defiance towards those around you. Instead, choose to break through your fear and respond positively. When rejected, react positively to others, breaking your habit of being silent or isolating yourself by not isolating yourself and feeling sorry for yourself. We talk to those close to us before it's too late. Expressing ourselves to others avoids expecting them to read our minds. We can talk honestly with others or spouses and avoid being controlled. We can ask them if they feel trapped or controlled because we talk openly and honestly. Growing means being able to handle feedback from others without fear.

While teaching about silent defiance, a staff member at a youth rehab center gave me a life-changing lesson. They struggled and disliked disciplining or confronting the rebellious youth unwilling to obey the program's rules. The leader encouraged them to approach the dilemma with love and care instead of confrontation. Seeing the need to improve as a caring act helps people to address weaknesses in others without getting angry or frustrated, and it is 'Carefrontation' instead of confrontation.

Overcoming fears can prevent rejected people from shutting down and help them communicate with their loved ones. Breaking our silence and speaking up shows our maturity and self-control rather than self-pity. We have deep discussions that can get intense and surprise others. As our environment changes, we find it less frustration-driven by anger and emotional explosions. People change how they talk to loved ones to show they care. We build good marriages through good communication and not defiance.

INSPIRE

PROMOTING PROMPT CORRECTION

When faced with rejection, the tendency to respond with silent defiance can be pervasive. However, it is crucial to avoid succumbing to this harmful behavior by resisting the urge and instead embracing the value of promptly correcting others or spouses in a caring manner to foster a culture of open communication. This approach not only preserves relationships but also inspires positive change and growth.

RESISTING CONTROL THROUGH SILENCE

Silent defiance has the potential to become a toxic tool for controlling others and our loved ones. To prevent this insidious dynamic from taking root, individuals should consciously refrain from using silent defiance and discourage it. When we avoid using silence to manipulate, we help foster healthier relationships based on respect and understanding.

CULTIVATING CORRECTIVE COMMUNICATION

An essential aspect of avoiding silent defiance involves teaching others or our spouses how to correct others with the right attitude instead of resorting to harmful silence. We can learn constructive ways to address issues and convey concerns. Cultivating a positive communication mindset is essential for resolving conflicts openly and productively and strengthening interpersonal connections.

People who have faced rejection challenges and overcome defiance inspire others to communicate openly instead of holding back and causing a more significant issue later. They help them speak up and be open to correcting others. They seek permission before talking to others to avoid being overpowering. Before giving advice or correcting others, they ensure their motives are pure and not driven by frustration or irritation. They are inspired to correct others at the right time and with the right motivation, and they do so without being controlling or angry.

We inspire those facing rejection challenges not to use silence to manipulate others into responding to them by saying nothing. Instead of using silence to manipulate others, we inspire them by demonstrating its negative power. By sharing our experiences, we inspire others to express their emotions and acknowledge their feelings. As they are sensitive to the feelings of others, they ask for permission to speak the truth to them. Inspiring them to communicate respectfully by asking for permission before speaking helps maintain relationships. It helps to inspire them to communicate respectfully and maintain relationships by asking for permission before speaking. Being inspired to confront negative behavior with care and concern.

We inspire them to show others their negative behavior, preventing them from doing something wrong that could hurt others. We show them how harmful, destructive behavior can be when they don't speak up to help others recognize and overcome their issues. Inspiring them to point out blind spots to others and respectfully helping them change. We inspire people to work on their weaknesses and believe solid relationships are crucial to overcoming obstacles. Inspiring them to set good examples by valuing their relationships with others. This results in a joyful celebration of everyone's efforts instead of being overpowering and controlling. We inspire others to work confidently and without fear by fostering a positive environment. By building solid relationships, they can give and receive constructive criticism.

CONCLUSION

Speaking up and being honest with others helped me stop controlling others and make sure a caring heart motivated me instead of being angry and frustrated when reaching out to help them. Instead of being controlling in my interactions with people, I became caring enough to talk to them before it was too late. Their response to my 'care-frontation,' not confrontation, was very positive. Their positive reaction freed me from my fear of correcting others. It then led me to do it more without being overpowering or controlling. This breakthrough over my silent defiance transformed how I worked with others, and I could correct them as I should.

APPLICATION

1. How do you respond when you need to correct others you fear may reject you?

2. Why do we need others to help us see our faults?

3. What pattern do we break When we stop using silent defiance?

4. What happens to your attitude to correction to others and theirs to you changes?

5. What do you understand by carefrontation versus confrontation?

CHAPTER NINE
CHALLENGE OF RESISTANCE

In a reflective moment, I recalled a friend's concerned words. "Bradley, you must slow down and catch your breath." I could hear the urgency and deep concern in their voice. They said, "You are going non-stop continually at a hundred miles an hour." However, my response at the time could have been more receptive. I shrugged off their caring advice with a dismissive remark, "This is how my parents and I function – constantly going at full speed." In my state of exhaustion, I failed to grasp the sincerity behind their words and overlooked the valuable correction they were offering. It was a missed opportunity to sit down, listen, and understand their genuine concern for my well-being.

BREAKDOWN

OVERREACTING TO CORRECTION

The broader challenge of performance often intertwines with accepting discipline or correction. This link can make it arduous for individuals to allow others to speak into their lives constructively. One typical response is to overreact defensively, manifesting in sarcasm and defensiveness. This defensive stance can hinder personal and professional growth, creating a barrier to valuable insights that could lead to improvement.

VICTIM MENTALITY AND OVERREACTIONS

Another obstacle in navigating the rejection challenge of correction is the tendency to adopt a victim mentality.

When faced with disciplinary actions or correction, individuals may feel trapped, fostering anger and overreactions. This victim mindset inhibits personal development and contributes to a negative cycle of unproductive responses to correction, hindering the ability to learn and adapt.

DISHONORING AND STUBBORNNESS

A significant consequence of struggling with the rejection challenge of correction is dishonoring and disrespecting those offering it. This can manifest as stubbornness and an unwillingness to listen, shutting down valuable avenues for personal and professional growth. Refrain from acknowledging constructive criticism to avoid stagnation, hindering the development of a teachable and adaptable mindset.

As rejected people, we perceive all forms of disciplinary correction as a personal rejection. We battle with being open to receiving from others who want to show us our faults that need to be changed. When someone tries to correct us, we overreact by ignoring, defending ourselves, or getting angry. If nothing works, we use sarcasm to make them stop talking about it. We often react negatively when someone gives us advice instead of thanking them and being open to discussion. As a result, we usually take much longer to see our weaknesses and only deal with them when we are ready to, instead of receiving the help offered promptly. If we had heeded the wise advice of people who could see our blind spots much better than we could, we could have saved ourselves a lot of pain and unnecessary time.

When we resist accepting discipline, we inadvertently cast ourselves as victims, wallowing in self-pity. In such a state, there's a risk of resorting to manipulation and intimidation if others fail to respond as we wish. The inclination to adopt a victim mindset persists even when someone attempts to correct us with kindness, misinterpreting it as dishonor or disrespect. Rather than perceiving the correction to help and strengthening, we may mistakenly believe that others intend to hurt and reject us.

This defensive reaction, rooted in past hurts from those who have rejected us, particularly figures of authority, unfolds as a recurring theme in our lives. The lingering scars from these rejection challenges contribute to our development of stubbornness, rendering us unteachable and resistant to further advice or corrections. The stubborn individual fiercely defends their perception of what is right, treating it as an untouchable "idol" that no one can challenge. This defensive stance becomes a barrier to personal growth and openness to learning.

BREAKTHROUGH

EMBRACING TEACHABILITY

The breakthrough in overcoming the rejection challenge of resisting discipline and correction occurs when individuals consciously decide to become teachable. This involves recognizing the distinctions between discipline, correction, and rejection. To reach this point, individuals must place a value on constructive correction and understand its potential for personal and professional growth. Fostering an environment where individuals can receive caring and wise advice without the defensive shield of sarcasm requires crucial elements such as openness, honesty, and transparency.

OVERCOMING SELF-PITY

Another crucial aspect of this breakthrough involves acknowledging and overcoming self-pity and a victim mentality. Instead of reacting with anger and defensiveness, individuals learn to wait and respond in an honoring way. By resisting the pull of victimhood, they create space for personal reflection and constructive responses to correction, ultimately breaking free from the negative cycle of overreactions.

CULTIVATING BEING TEACHABLE

The key to conquering this rejection challenge is to remain open to learning. This means a willingness to learn from others and to let go of stubborn attachments to personal beliefs or idols. By embracing a teachable mindset, individuals open themselves to continuous learning and improvement, fostering a positive cycle of growth and adaptability.

To navigate our personal growth effectively, we must distinguish between discipline, correction, and rejection. Often, our emotions cloud our ability to recognize our weaknesses and blind spots. When someone genuinely cares about us, they correct us and intend to assist us in improvement. These corrections help us change destructive behaviors and mindsets without rejecting us as individuals.

Valuing the guidance of those who care means being open to making changes based on their corrections. Breaking down our defense mechanisms like sarcasm allows us to engage in open and honest self-reflection. In this vulnerable state, when someone encourages us to draw closer rather than pushing us away in fear or anger, we become more receptive to listening and heeding their counsel or correction. Through this understanding, we foster an environment for constructive growth and positive change.

To overcome this rejection challenge, we shouldn't feel sorry for ourselves or try to control those who want to help us improve. We need to express our emotions to those who correct us without overreacting like we used to when we felt hurt. It requires self-discipline and self-control to take the time to wait and think about what we are telling us before reacting. When we feel pressured to respond, we should immediately say, "Thank you for telling me that. Can I take some time to think about it and get back to you later on?" This prevents us from making an immediate emotional response and allows us to go to trusted ones we have permitted to speak into our lives and see what we think about it. Acting without proper preparation can cause harm to us or others. Learning to control our emotions and patience helps us avoid offending those who correct us or point out our flaws.

Waiting and cooling down can prevent us from becoming angry and aggressive in our reactions. Waiting before reacting helps us overcome feeling like a victim and choose a calm response. Being open about something that could harm us and our relationships with others deserves recognition. We honor ourselves by letting ourselves share precisely what we perceive without trying to control us with the wrong response. We then show ourselves the respect we are due for boldly addressing our concerns. It is crucial to appreciate whether we are right or wrong; it was of deep enough concern to us that we took our precious time to speak to each other about it.

Being receptive to feedback and open to change can help us overcome stubbornness and being unteachable. We can break through by listening to others and getting confirmation from our trusted advisors. We show humility by accepting correction and letting go of our stubborn idols. Only when we see the truth about something we unknowingly do wrong can we change our attitude toward it. It took me several months to realize that I needed to slow down and take a break, as suggested by my caring friend. I naturally worked on the problems that caused performance issues. It took me years to break the habit, even after recognizing its impact. I fell into a pattern of constantly saying: "I'll do that."

INSPIRE

DISTINGUISHING CORRECTIONS

Encouraging individuals to respond correctly to correction starts with distinguishing between correction, discipline, and rejection. By fostering this understanding, people can approach corrective feedback with clarity, recognizing the nuances of each and avoiding unnecessary defensiveness. A positive atmosphere for corrective discipline, where sarcasm is absent, promotes a better response to feedback.

DEVELOPING AN OVERCOMER MINDSET

Inspiring individuals to express themselves when they feel trapped, coupled with cultivating an overcomer mindset, paves the way for honor and respect in the face of correction. By acknowledging their rejection challenges and embracing a proactive approach to overcoming them, individuals can shift away from victim mentalities. This shift fosters personal growth and contributes to a culture of mutual respect within interpersonal relationships.

PRACTICING PATIENCE AND LISTENING

An integral part of responding correctly to correction involves inspiring individuals to exercise patience and to actively listen before reacting negatively. Waiting to absorb the feedback and understanding its context allows for a more thoughtful response. This practice leads to a genuine appreciation for the value of correction, fostering a mindset that embraces continuous improvement and values the input of others.

We inspire people by showing the actual value of correction when it is done with the right heart and attitude. Helping them understand that corrections coming from a place of care are not rejection. Inspiring them to check their motives to be sure they are correcting people in love and not trying to control or hurt them. We aim to inspire them to be receptive to others' constructive criticism. Prompting them to process information, such as using sarcasm, before reacting negatively.

We will inspire people to express their feelings freely regarding what they have said to them without attempting to defend themselves. Their questions will be harmless, promote open discussion, and prevent them from feeling trapped or victimized. We inspire them to overcome their rejection challenges over time as they see how to change their mindset. When they give feedback with the right motive, they inspire others to value and welcome correction—seeing how correction can be one of the most freeing things for them. With the help of correction, they can move past the weaknesses they have been blinded to. We will inspire people to speak the truth boldly to others with no fear as long as they do it in a caring and loving manner and with no hidden agenda. When done correctly, it replaces disrespect with genuine respect.

The goal is to inspire people to respond only once they are calm and not offended. We inspire them to create space to ponder what they've heard or think they've heard. We inspire them to value helping others through correction without becoming overly defensive and to reach out to those they trust to help them process what we've heard without getting overly emotional.

CONCLUSION

When I finally saw how important it was to receive correction and not label it as rejection, my life became much more prosperous and productive. If someone outside my trusted circle corrects me, I thank them for their words and choose not to respond or overreact negatively. Instead, I will say, "Can I think about what you've said and get back to you?" I give myself time to think about it and cool down if what they've said angers me. Or I might say, "Before I react negatively to what you've said, can I talk it over with my trusted confidants and then get back to you?" Using these responses, I avoid damaging my relationship with the person who corrected me and show them I value their feedback.

APPLICATION

1. What feelings come up for you when someone corrects you?

2. Who can you turn to when you feel trapped by someone who has corrected you?

3. How willing are you to learn from trusted people around you?

4. What steps can you take to stop you from overreacting to correction?

5. What benefits can you see from allowing others to correct you?

CHAPTER TEN
CHALLENGE OF RETALIATING

Flashback: "I am doing my best!" I yelled out as I burst into tears. I struggled to take down notes dictated to us by our teacher due to my cerebral palsy. My inability to write notes as quickly as my fellow students trapped me. It was an ongoing battle for me as I went through school. Despite developing my shorthand method and using it as much as possible, I still broke down, unsure how to keep up as I should. These experiences made me feel trapped, resulting in my struggling to relate as well as I should have to those in authority over me. I had to learn to openly and honestly express my struggles without rebelling and rejecting their authority.

BREAKDOWN

OVERREACTION IN DISAGREEMENT

When faced with rejection from those in authority, individuals often overreact when met with disagreement. This heightened emotional response can lead to impulsive reactions and an intense backlash against perceived rejection. The emotional intensity in these situations may cloud judgment, hindering constructive dialogue and cooperation.

REBELLION THROUGH OVER-PERFORMANCE

Another typical response to rejection is rebellion expressed through over-performance. To prove oneself or seek acknowledgment, individuals may demonstrate actions beyond expectations. This behavior can be a coping mechanism driven by a desire to gain validation or recognition from those in authority, even if it means surpassing established boundaries.

STUBBORNNESS AND DISRESPECT

Repeated rejection challenges can lead to a stubborn and unteachable attitude, creating a barrier to constructive communication. Individuals may need guidance and feedback, deteriorating their relationship with authority figures. This resistance often translates into a display of dishonor and disrespect, contributing to a negative cycle of strained interactions and diminished mutual understanding.

Disagreeing with authority or having unpleasant experiences with authority figures can cause overreactions. Resolving issues with others is crucial before projecting our anger onto someone else. Our negativity causes us to build walls that break down our relationship before we even try working together. Past conflicts influence our fear of authority, with people in authority who reject us for our adverse reactions. Suspicion of driving others gives too much power over us, leading to our control because we fear rejection if we do not comply.

This driving fear of not being able to comply as we should cause us to over-perform without setting the healthy boundaries we should. Because we desire to please those in authority, we go from one extreme to another, which is unhealthy. We do way more than we should to please, honor, or respect others. Our efforts bring to the surface many of the issues we looked at in the performance storm in section one. If we think we're unhappy with our work, we might get upset and cause more problems. Feeling controlled or driven by others, we become more stubborn and defiant in responding to us.

Motivated by fear and a desire for control, we often find ourselves entangled in rebellious and stubborn behaviors as our past wounds obscure our perception and inflict pain. In this state, we become resistant to hearing the well-intentioned words of others, showcasing a surprising disrespect or disobedience that perplexes us. Unaware of the underlying struggles we are presently facing or the lingering impact of past hurts from family, teachers, bosses, or friends, we build walls around ourselves. These walls, coupled with our stubbornness and resistance to being taught, create a challenge in expressing our emotions without succumbing to overwhelming emotions.

The difficulty lies in our hesitance to communicate our feelings openly, a struggle made worse by the scars of our past. This hesitation often persists until it is too late, and we respond with tears or confusing emotions that elude our understanding until we finally open up.

BREAKTHROUGH

PAUSE, REFLECT, AND SEEK COUNSEL

To effectively navigate conflicts with authority, it is crucial to adopt a deliberate approach. Taking a moment to pause, reflect on the situation, and seek advice from trusted counselors can provide valuable perspectives. These things allow for a more thoughtful response, reducing the likelihood of reacting impulsively or emotionally.

COMMUNICATION AND SELF-REFLECTION

A key strategy involves learning to respond by asking ourselves challenging questions and fostering openness to discussing underlying concerns. By engaging in honest self-reflection and open communication, we create a foundation for constructive dialogue that facilitates a better understanding of our motivations and those of the authority figure.

AVOID OVERWORKING AND REBELLION

Overworking and rebellious tendencies can exacerbate conflicts. Learning not to overburden ourselves and avoiding the temptation to rebel against authority is essential. Balancing, asserting individual perspectives, and maintaining respect for authority helps create a more harmonious dynamic.

HONOR AUTHORITY

Embracing a receptive attitude towards correction is vital for personal growth. Being open to learning, honoring, respecting, and obeying those in authority fosters a positive and cooperative environment. This attitude promotes a healthier exchange of ideas and enhances the overall effectiveness of working relationships.

We should train ourselves not to overreact when we disagree with authority and ask ourselves tough questions, like, "Why am I reacting this way? What is triggering my reaction? Have I been open and honest with you about my feelings and what's happening within me? Am I reacting this way because of past unresolved issues with someone in authority?" Doing this allows us to escape being trapped with nowhere for help. We must approach the right people to help to resolve the issues we have realized. It's important to submit it to someone who has also submitted it so we have a support system when faced with unsolvable problems. We must recognize and tear down any walls built using the tools discussed in Chapter One.

We need to know when we're overworking ourselves to please others and ensure our motivation comes from the right place. We must stop ourselves the minute we feel driven by any fear of those we are under, whether it's family, teachers, or bosses. To control our responses toward those requesting our help, we must learn to stop, wait, and listen when we detect fear driving us. We must set clear boundaries when serving others and avoid becoming too dependent on them. We should also communicate what we will do for them. Our ability to judge things may differ based on our experiences and how much we've healed.

Overcoming past struggles and fears is pivotal in fostering a mindset that welcomes and respects authority figures. To achieve humility, it becomes imperative to shed erroneous beliefs, allowing us to be accountable to those in positions of authority. This accountability, coupled with the practice of honor, respect, and obedience, catalyzes recognition of our inherent value and worth.

Before willingly placing ourselves under someone's authority, it is prudent to introspect and ask, "To whose authority do you submit?" This introspective inquiry guides us, showing where we can turn if we ever feel trapped, threatened, or controlled. Ensuring the person, we answer to comprehend the submission experience provides peace of mind. This shared understanding reduces the likelihood of abusing authority for control or harm, fostering an environment characterized by mutual respect and consideration.

INSPIRE

PRACTICE PATIENCE

Encourage individuals to overcome conflicts with authority by emphasizing the importance of patience and thoughtful responses. Share the lesson of learning to wait before reacting impulsively and the value of asking critical questions instead of succumbing to overreactions. This approach fosters a more constructive and understanding relationship with authority figures.

AVOID FEAR-DRIVEN OVERWORKING

Advocate against letting fear compel individuals to overwork. Share personal breakthroughs highlighting the detrimental effects of excessive workload driven by fear. By addressing this aspect, individuals can find a healthier balance in their professional and personal lives, leading to improved relationships with authority figures.

BE TEACHABLE HUMBLE SHOWING RESPECT

Inspire those around you by highlighting the profound importance of embracing a teachable and humble demeanor while demonstrating honor, respect, and obedience. Share personal experiences and breakthroughs highlighting the positive impact of adopting these values. Encouraging a mindset that values continuous learning and respectful collaboration can contribute to more harmonious interactions with authority figures.

We inspire others to change their view of authority to avoid overreacting in frustrating situations. We inspire people to ask themselves tough questions before reacting, to wait, listen, and hear what they need through their answers and those they consult. This will help them respond appropriately. We inspire them to cool off and release frustration, woundedness, or anger. Answering correctly will prevent emotional reactions that are potentially harmful to themselves and others.

Before getting married, I used to react impulsively. I learned to type out my response when I was angry. Then, I had someone I trusted to read and edit it before I sent it or talked to the person. Since being married, I have discussed an issue with my wife and get her reaction and wise input before I respond to the person. It's important not to let anger destroy our relationship when others don't follow our advice. We can ask to discuss the issue with the person we answer to. We can discuss the matter calmly without letting our past encounters with authority affect our behavior toward the person in charge. Sometimes, this last step is impossible. For instance, I couldn't tell the principal about my teacher. I should have discussed my issue with the teacher and asked how to work together on the problem. These practical principles can help us build strong and positive relationships with people in authority or those who work with us.

We inspire others to reevaluate the motivation behind their work and discourage overworking driven by the fear of rejection from superiors. Leaders can set an example by giving their best and fostering team independence. Encouraging individuals to establish boundaries and recognize limits without fearing criticism or rejection, emphasizing the importance of maintaining a healthy work-life balance. Guiding others to prevent the escalation of internal conflicts or frustrations stemming from past hurts inflicted by those in power. We inspire others not to let these issues erode relationships, avoiding the construction of walls that hinder open and honest dialogue. By fostering an environment of understanding, collaboration, and empathy, we can inspire them to approach their work with purpose and autonomy, contributing to a more balanced and fulfilling professional journey.

Our actions can inspire others to be teachable and receptive to authority figures, regardless of their personal views. We can inspire people to break down any pre-set ways they may have stubbornly allowed to develop in their mindsets. Those in charge should identify the pre-set ways more quickly and address them. We inspire people to see how their mindsets may have led them into silent, subtle, or open rebellion and acknowledge their pre-set fierce defense. We inspire them to show humility by acknowledging this and asking authority figures to hold them accountable in the future. As a result, it inspires them to obey and respect those in authority over them by not allowing themselves to be controlled by their superiors.

CONCLUSION

Respecting authority figures includes family, friends, school, work, and government. Working with people in authority is a part of life; we cannot escape it. We must acknowledge it is like gravity and will be part of our lives until we die. It's essential to respect and obey those in authority, even if they have hurt us in the past. The exception to this is abusive authority and power.

I struggled to follow authority because of my experiences with hurtful people in authority. A father figure who understood authority issues changed my perspective on submission. He did not force me into building a deeper relationship by coming under his authority. Instead, he said, "Let us simply walk together in a relationship and, over time, see how it develops," and said, "Here is the number of the man I am submitted to. "If you ever feel you cannot resolve an issue with me, please contact him."

Years later, as we were teaching together, I was not too happy about a situation I found myself in. As I talked to him about it, his answer was jokingly: "Better you than me." I didn't immediately respond, but a short while later, I said, "What's the number of the man over you? I want to call him." We laughed together and talked through the issue, which was nothing major. For years after that, we would look at each other occasionally and say, "What's his number again?" as we laughed together. What a joy to find a friend to help me overcome my fear of authority! And what a pleasure to value, honor, respect, and obey those in authority, seeing how it has increased my authority as I teach and work with others daily.

APPLICATION

1. What past hurts, wounds or rejection may block you from embracing those in authority over you?

2. Are you willing to release those and start afresh, giving honor to and seeing yourself come into a more significant place of authority?

3. Why is it important to only submit to rightly aligned people?

4. What attitudes rise when you feel controlled by those in authority?

5. What steps can prevent us from letting the wrong attitudes develop

SECTION THREE

OVER-ANALYZING

CHAPTER ELEVEN
THE CHALLENGE OF DISDAIN

"Hey, I noticed your unique way of moving and speaking. Can you share more about it? Here's your backpack; come over if you want to pick it up."

This is what some of my classmates yelled at me as they began running off with my book bag. Their bullying provoked me to run away as quickly as possible. The longer I ran, the more they mocked and laughed at me until they finally dropped it and ran off laughing at me. This kind of thing happened to me continually, especially when I started attending a regular public school. Hearing those words daily made me eventually believe maybe I was a spastic flawed retard. Therefore, I did not like who I was. I was mad that I had become the school clown for everyone to mock and tease. The longer I believed the lie that there was something seriously wrong with the way I was, the more I rejected myself.

BREAKDOWN

EXTERNAL PROGRAMMING FOR SELF-WORTH

Individuals often grapple with the rejection challenge of disdain due to external influences that dictate their values and identity based on societal expectations. This struggle is not unique to any specific condition but extends to various reasons, such as physical appearance or perceived shortcomings.

NEGATIVE SELF-TALK AND STRUGGLES

The internal dialogue of negative self-talk can contribute significantly to bitterness and anger, leading individuals to despise their abilities. This self-critical mindset may arise from societal pressures, personal insecurities, or the impact of external judgments.

PERFORMANCE-DRIVEN EXPECTATIONS

The relentless pursuit of perfection and the fear of making mistakes create a toxic cycle where individuals feel driven to perform at all costs. This performance-driven mentality often results in a deep-seated aversion to errors and a constant battle for receiving compliments or acknowledgment. This further brings on feelings of disdain.

The words and actions of those around us can influence us, so we lose sight of our value. Listening to wrong words can make us doubt ourselves, believing others more than ourselves. The longer these thoughts stay in our minds, the more difficult it becomes to break through, thus disdaining ourselves. If we cannot see what is happening soon enough, we will battle to know what is true. This often leads to us believing in the lies more than the truths about ourselves. Others' actions or reactions can intensify this. Overcoming negative thoughts about oneself can become more challenging because of other people's opinions about us.

Persisting challenges can increasingly impact our self-perception, fostering negativity in how we view ourselves. External factors, alongside internal struggles, contribute to the scarring of our self-esteem. Contemporary issues like obesity often lead individuals to reject themselves.

Also, societal expectations, such as choosing a college major for acceptance, can become performances that shape self-worth.

For instance, a young lady's relentless pursuit of academic success to please her father resulted in straight a's in college. However, his dismissive response was, "I'm sorry college was so easy." His response shattered her self-esteem, eventually leading her down a troubling path. The impact of others' reactions to our efforts, whether in sports, academics, or work, can significantly mold our self-image.

Recognize that whatever instigates disdain within us needs swift acknowledgment and resolution. This shift is crucial. Failure to address these sources promptly may result in negative programming of our minds, poisoning our mindset. Believing falsehoods about ourselves can lead to hopelessness, undermining our intrinsic value and rendering life seemingly meaningless.

Seeking our identity solely from others' reactions, acceptance, or rejection can lead us astray from a genuine understanding of ourselves. The more that others reject us, instead of accepting us for who we are, the more we struggle with disdain. Today's young people find themselves rejected by their fathers, especially in their teenage years. Our father's rejection profoundly affects our lives and self-value. Our lack of fatherly words of affirmation or acceptance shapes our futures negatively. The absence of fathers in children's lives is causing adverse effects on their identity and well-being.

As families break down, single parents raise children, causing us to lack the balance a father and mother should provide. Fathers usually speak the truth, while mothers speak comfort to their children. If children accidentally cut themselves, the father may scold them for bleeding on the rug. However, Mom says: "Come now, let me take care of your boo-boo."

Children need both perspectives to live in reality and recognize truth and grace. One without the other causes us to live in unreality about the truth. Unreality makes us feel we can do whatever we like, knowing the Band-Aid will always be there. To always have a Band-Aid, we need to be more responsible and accept the consequences of our actions. How others around us, especially our parents and close peers, behave and speak profoundly affects us. When girls feel they are not pretty or loved enough by their fathers, rejection enters. When boys think they are not fitting in with the crowd and performing well enough for their parents, rejection enters. Rejection by others leads to disdain for ourselves.

When we don't like ourselves, we may speak badly about ourselves when we think no one is around. A destructive pattern of negative self-talk can then grow. Developing a pattern so strong that eventually, we do it without even thinking about it. As I continually heard my peers calling me a spastic retard and mocking me for my slow movements and speech, I believed that was who I was. Eventually, anger consumed me as I resented how people treated me, and I started showing negative emotions towards those who rejected me. The continued rejection made me not want to be around others, as I intensely disliked myself.

My disdain resulted in me despising my abilities and talents. This disdain also caused me to become blind to my strengths and what I could offer others. I began showing disdain towards how sensitive I could be towards others and my ability to pick up on others' hurts or needs. I didn't like being sensitive because it made me feel like a clown for all to laugh at. My sensitivity caused me to overact by reacting more than others usually would, giving them great laughs. Their laughter caused even greater disdain and self-rejection.

We react with performance to break through our disdain. Performance is a challenge we have recognized several times in our journey together. We will further address it before we are done. A tool we used to gain self-acceptance is performance. Thinking our performance will make us feel accepted and approved of. Through our performance, we try as hard as possible to get our self-acceptance, value, and worth from our achievements. We fall into a deadly trap of trying to gain acceptance and value through our performance.

Performance challenge issues arise if we fail or feel rejected despite our efforts. We view ourselves based on our achievements or the actions, reactions, and words of others. Our value, worth, acceptance, and identity should come from our fathers or mothers. When we gain our identity through how we function, we run into problems. These problems often surface in our workplace and affect how we react positively or negatively to our co-workers. Our adverse reactions to others surprise them because we don't realize we feel rejected. Getting our worth, value, and identity from what we do is an enormous problem in the workplace today. When we get our worth, value, and identity from what we do, we become overly protective of our title, defending it. We become tricked into believing our title should come from how we function instead of who we are. People who thought I could not teach rejected me. They judged me for my slow speech, actions, and reactions because of my cerebral palsy, judging a book by its cover before reading it.

However, as my teaching ability grew and people recognized it, I filled up my schedule for almost eighteen months. I used to identify myself by my popularity as a teacher until someone came into my life and reminded me that my job wasn't my true identity. As I pondered his wisdom, I discovered I function as a teacher, and people enjoy listening to me, but teaching is not who I am. Teaching is how I operate. People must enjoy what I do and who I am as a friend. People can fall in love with your gift or work accomplishments, ignoring who you are. You can be outstanding in your work but not be someone your co-workers can relate to. Can your co-workers relate to you as a trusted friend and with what you do? This is an important question to ask yourself periodically.

Low self-esteem makes us tough on ourselves for making errors or doing things imperfectly. (Perfectionism is one of the ultimate challenges we will address later). In an earlier chapter, I gave a great example, showing how I beat myself up with negative self-talk for dropping an egg by mistake. When the man heard what I was saying, when I dropped the egg, he spoke sternly to correct me. His stern words surprised me at first, as it had become second nature for me to reject myself whenever I made a mistake or did not do something as well as I wanted to. His stern, caring words of concern helped me to become more sensitive to what I was saying about myself and how I responded to my mistakes.

Those struggling with disdain battle to receive compliments from others. When we receive praise, we have a hard time accepting it instead of receiving it as we should. We feel we are not good enough to be celebrated or to receive praise from others. Our fake humility and pride prevent us from getting the thanks we deserve. We should thank others for acknowledging our abilities. Our disdainful rejection of ourselves makes it hard to thank those celebrating us.

BREAKTHROUGH

RECOGNIZING OUR INHERENT VALUE

The first step to breaking through disdain involves acknowledging our intrinsic value. This requires a conscious effort to recognize and challenge our internalized lies, fostering an acceptance of the truth about our uniqueness. By dismantling false beliefs, we pave the way for a more positive self-perception.

POSITIVE SELF-TALK

Listening to our internal dialogue is essential. Breaking through disdain involves actively engaging with our self-talk, identifying negative patterns, and letting go of detrimental feelings. Embracing our strengths and redirecting self-talk towards positivity contributes significantly to building a healthier self-image.

MOVING BEYOND PERFORMANCE

The journey to overcoming disdain includes a shift from a performance-driven mindset. Instead of constantly striving to meet external expectations, getting value from lessons and focusing on personal growth is crucial. By learning from experiences and accepting compliments graciously, we break free from the confines of constant performance and cultivate a more authentic self-worth.

We need the support of others to realize others' actions or reactions should not define our worth. We learn not to let rejection define us and seek guidance from positive role models to see our true potential. By choosing to surround ourselves with these positive influences, we find it easier to be rooted in the truth about ourselves instead of the lies. Instead of believing the lies or mistruths of others, we believe the truth. Individuals who have experienced hurt often perpetuate this pain by inflicting harm on others, and those who have faced rejection may reject others. (We will delve deeper into addressing this challenge later.) Having supportive and encouraging individuals as cheerleaders can play a crucial role in empowering people to embrace their authentic selves and foster confidence.

We thank our cheerleaders by saying: "Thanks for helping me see who I am and pointing out my uniqueness. I am not changing the things I have no control over. Instead, I will change what I can without allowing others to shape who I am any longer." My life changed forever from the night I embraced who I was at eighteen. Two weeks after embracing who I was, a fellow student called me a spastic retard. I ignored him and continued doing my best without negatively reacting as I had in the past. When he came and apologized to me later, I said: "Thank you for coming to apologize. I can't change the way I function because of my cerebral palsy.

I'm changing how I see myself and how my actions affect people who don't understand me." My breakthrough gave me a greater victory over my adverse reactions to those rejecting or mocking me. We must accept ourselves and focus on enjoying our achievements. This includes not fearing people who don't understand us, regardless of age.

Positive words from fathers can help us overcome negative feelings. Affirmation from others can help us find our true identity and change our mindset. Our transformation frees us from the tormenting lies we have believed for years. This freedom of having our minds renewed and transformed takes time and requires patience. Overcoming self-disdain requires patience and developing positive mindsets. Renewal of our disdain-filled attitudes depends on the number of lies we or others have spoken over us. The greater the number of lies believed, the greater the truth needed to replace them.

For eighteen years, I held a steadfast belief that I was a person with cerebral palsy, labeling myself as someone with significant challenges and issues. The depth to which I had internalized these falsehoods required time for the truth to permeate—acknowledging that I was not defective, purposeless goods. It became necessary to embrace the reality that it did not define me; I could aspire to become the person I desired. The revelation of my true identity, free from disdain, was a profoundly liberating experience. Instead of viewing myself through the lens of a "spastic retard," I saw a young man with a bright future.

This newfound perspective allowed me to shed disdain toward others and cultivate sensitivity. Recognizing the positive aspects of what I had previously perceived as unfavorable, I became more adept at guiding others to embrace their unique qualities. We need to replace negative self-talk with positivity. Our positive thinking causes us to pay closer attention to our speech and how we talk to ourselves privately or in public. When we fill ourselves with self-disdain, we quickly recognize it—not letting it continue by reaching out for help from others to break any cycle of negative self-disdain. Reaching out to trusted people can help us break free. Reaching out to the right people protects us from growing anger, bitterness, or resentment, leading to less self-disdain.

We find it easier to forgive others than we do to forgive ourselves. Forgiving ourselves is challenging when we are harboring self-disdain. We are very hard on ourselves when we make even the most minor mistakes. Our mistakes cause our self-disdain to deepen if we do not see what is going on soon enough. We must fully embrace our uniqueness and talents to overcome our self-disdain. I was angry and resentful towards those who rejected or belittled me because of my cerebral palsy. I had to overcome it by fully accepting and embracing my uniqueness and talents.

My self-disdain closed my eyes to my individuality and skills. However, after I forgave those who had caused me to believe lies about myself, I felt like a different person in my mind and heart. My view of myself radically changed as my mind and heart changed. Learning to accept myself changed how I treated others. I went from being angry and bitter towards them to having compassion. My compassion replaced my despising of others. My understanding caused me to ask myself why I was reacting negatively, and I thought about how I could help rather than reject them.

By accepting and embracing our unique way of functioning, we overcome self-disdain. Knowing the differences between how we function and who we are enables us to view how we work with others differently. This discernment helps us break free of our tendencies to gain acceptance and approval through our work. Our understanding enables us to function uniquely without being concerned about how people choose to respond to us. Our only concern is to make sure we uniquely do what we should do the best we can by putting our all into it. We function the best we can at our job, knowing our job is what we do, not who we are. Our ability to discern this helps us to surround ourselves with those who know how to relate to how we function apart from who we are. We then regularly check in to see which co-workers respond to how we work and who wants to relate to us as friends.

Acknowledging our successes can raise our self-esteem and reduce our worry about failure. We replace our fear of making mistakes and beating up on ourselves with valuing who we are. We can see how much richer we can become through lessons from our mistakes. By valuing learning from our mistakes, we allow ourselves to embrace life. Embracing our life lessons frees us from trying as hard as possible to prevent ourselves from making mistakes. We use our mistakes as building blocks instead of stumbling blocks. We can use these experiences to help others.

Looking back at my life, I do not regret what I went through growing up with cerebral palsy. I regret not recognizing the valuable life lessons of my cerebral palsy sooner. My pain and others' words prevented me from seeing how these lessons have molded my character. My blindness hindered me from seeing how to make lemonade from my lemons (my rejection challenge). Making lemonade helped me learn to help others do the same with our lemons (rejection challenges). As I mentioned in my introduction to our journey, it was only a few years ago I had the mindset change. My wife encouraged me to see all the positive things my unique challenges had produced in me instead of staying focused on the negative areas. We can accept compliments without feeling proud or dismissing them. Express gratitude for compliments by thanking those who supported and guided you to achieve success.

INSPIRE

SELF-ACCEPTANCE AND VALUE

We inspire others to value their intrinsic worth, not merely focus on their capabilities. Teaching them to embrace their belief in their uniqueness and operate from that authentic understanding of themselves. By acknowledging and celebrating who we are, we set a powerful example for others to cultivate self-acceptance.

POSITIVELY LEVERAGING UNIQUE TALENTS

An essential step in inspiring self-acceptance involves attentive listening to our self-talk. Releasing negative emotions and embracing our unique talents contribute to building a positive self-image. By encouraging others to recognize and use their distinctive abilities, we foster an environment of self-empowerment.

ACCEPTANCE BEYOND ACHIEVEMENTS

Inspiring self-acceptance extends to understanding that acceptance comes from who we are, not just what we do. When we take the time to extract valuable lessons from our life experiences and relish compliments or being celebrated. We reinforce the idea that our self-worth is not based on our achievements.

We inspire others to accept themselves and their uniqueness. Accepting themselves and embracing their identity is essential for serving others. Accepting who they are releases them from the lies or mistruths they have believed. The longer they believe the truth, the more they accept themselves. Standing on the truth about who they are inspires them to stop disdaining their valuable uniqueness and realize how helpful they are, looking for fathers, mothers, and close friends to affirm them healthily. Knowing their value affects how they interact with others every day. Positive affirmations from the right people inspire them to accept themselves and function uniquely.

Their positive reprogramming inspires them to believe truth more than lies. Considering the truth opens their eyes to recognize their value and worth instead of letting our disdain rob it. Knowing their value and worth inspires us to share our uniqueness with others and expect nothing in return. We recognize the importance of our unique offerings and work hard to ensure we function correctly so that others can benefit from us. Seeing how we could rob others stops us from being selfish and fearful. We stop being selfish and give freely to anyone who would take it.

We inspire others to be mindful of their self-talk and how they treat others—listening to what they say about themselves continuously when they look at themselves in the mirror. They are paying attention to their words in public and private. By paying closer attention to their words, as well as the words of others, they can recognize themselves. As they learn to identify self-disdain signs, they become inspired to handle it effectively. Dealing with their disdain quickly and effectively helps them speak to themselves as they would talk to others. Being inspired to change what they can by paying attention to their mirror self-talk. They alter their self-talk by no longer criticizing their weaknesses.

Accepting their shortcomings and faults makes them less likely to feel angry, bitter, or resentful. Letting go of wrong self-beliefs prevents negative influence from others. The actions, reactions, and words of others no longer move them. Instead, they stand firm in their value, worth, and uniqueness despite others' actions, reactions, and words. They can stand firm, as they know how unique they are, knowing who has sent them and how they are to function.

Being inspired to recognize their worth and abilities gives them the confidence to work boldly. They can help others. To do the same by identifying and valuing their skills and abilities.

By overcoming their self-doubt, they inspire others and demonstrate that success is nothing to be afraid of. We consciously inspire them to resist the temptation of performing solely for acceptance and approval from others. It's essential to derive inspiration from the joy of performing and being acknowledged for being their authentic selves rather than seeking external approval. Being accepted for who they are, distinct from their daily functions or service to others, is a liberating realization. Understanding that their worth is not contingent on how they serve allows them to break free from ulterior motives. This right motivation propels them to refine their unique qualities and abilities, intending to assist others more effectively. As they focus on being genuinely helpful without hidden agendas, their functional skills naturally improve, leading to a more joyful and excellent execution of tasks.

Elevating their effectiveness and skill set allows them to extend assistance to others, fostering a collaborative environment. This cooperative spirit, grounded in their uniqueness and abilities, enhances their ability to impact those around them positively. They cultivate genuine friendships, making their interactions more enjoyable and inspiring them to be more helpful, celebrating their colleagues' unique qualities. Through their example, they can impart the wisdom of discerning the difference between the roles they play in their tasks and the essence of who they are as loyal friends.

Overcoming self-disdain, they inspire their peers to value their mistakes. Through loving their mistakes, they embrace themselves as they should. Embracing mistakes and life lessons allows them to be used for our benefit in the future. However, not only can we benefit from our mistakes, but they can also profoundly benefit others in the future by inspiring us to recognize how valuable our mistakes can be to ourselves and others. We pay closer attention to our self-talk when we look at ourselves in the mirror. Knowing that our self-talk reflects what we may need to change. Our self-talk shows how much work still needs to be done to overcome our self-disdain. It also shows us the lemons we have to make lemonade with.

We inspire others to find the good in their mistakes and use them to learn and grow. Having the correct perspective allows challenged people not to see lemons as a simply bitter fruit but as a great fruit to make lemonade and to help others. Individuals facing challenges find inspiration in accepting compliments by shifting their self-perception. Celebrating themselves and getting compliments helps them avoid false humility. Being thankful and receiving the affirmation of others protects from pride. They remain humble by being grateful and acknowledging others' compliments like a thank-you card. Accepting the help of others who have helped them, they humbly say thanks, which means: "I could not have done it without your help and encouragement."

CONCLUSION

It was a joy to embrace my uniqueness and accept who I was, not what others said I was. Instead of despising my cerebral palsy, I focused on how it could help me turn my weaknesses into strengths. I feared having to stand up and talk because of how others reacted; I did not want to talk. Yet today, I have to speak constantly as a teacher. I would not have written this book for you without getting over my self-disdain.

Self-disdain is an enormous challenge that many today face because of several factors. This challenge causes people to struggle to accept who they are and embrace their true identity. This challenge is something young people experience during their teenage years. Our self-disdain makes us battle with knowing who we are and what we are to be doing in the future. Older generations struggle to see our worth beyond our jobs or titles and seek validation through our achievements. We focus too much on doing instead of making ourselves struggle with self-acceptance and fulfillment.

APPLICATION

1. Where do you get your genuine sense of value and worth from?

2. What does your self-talk in the mirror reveal about how you see yourself?

3. Can you distinguish what you are to do from who you are and who relates to those in your life?

4. Who are your greatest cheerleaders and encouragers?

5. How well are you able to receive compliments from us?

CHAPTER TWELVE
THE CHALLENGE OF SELF-PITY

I wished I didn't have cerebral palsy so I could get the Eagle Award. My academic grades were good enough, and I was the head of the macrame club, but my sports achievements were not good enough. I worked hard for this award, but my cerebral palsy held me back. After hearing that I had not made it again, I began spiraling into self-pity; I felt sorry for myself, knowing I could not achieve what I needed. This became a familiar cycle for me, and it caused me to face the challenge of self-pity often. It is a challenge frequently encountered by those who battle with rejection.

BREAKDOWN

ISOLATION AND INTROSPECTION

Challenged individuals frequently encounter a tendency to isolate themselves, engaging in introspective reflections that may reinforce a sense of self-pity. This withdrawal can lead to a skewed perspective on relationships, as individuals may unintentionally employ ineffective methods of communication and connection.

CHILDISH BEHAVIOR AND NEGATIVITY

A typical response to rejection challenges is adopting childish behavior, focusing disproportionately on negative aspects, and avoiding expressions of honor. This mindset, often rooted in feeling like the underdog, can hinder personal growth and strain relationships as individuals become fixated on the hardships they face.

LACK OF SELF-RECOGNITION AND PESSIMISM

Challenged individuals may need help recognizing their strengths, leading to a pessimistic outlook. This negativity can manifest as jealousy and competitiveness, as individuals cannot appreciate their unique qualities and achievements, contributing to a cycle of self-doubt and discontent.

When challenged, we turn to isolation instead of seeking help. Thus, we become overly self-centered and introverted, which is unhealthy for us or others. Often, feeling sorry for ourselves, focusing on the wrong things, becoming victims, and focusing on what we can't do leads to self-pity. Our self-pity causes us to be overly focused on ourselves so that we do not see the needs of others. Our pitiful self-focus stops us from reaching out to those around us or being willing to help them. The longer we stay self-focused, the bigger our weaknesses seem to become, strengthening our challenge with self-pity. By dwelling negatively on ourselves continually, we lose focus on our strengths and what we can do. Our wrong focus causes us to get swept up in this rejection challenge and reminds us how little we can do. The lies we listen to program our thinking incorrectly.

Our wrong programming ties into this challenge, as we eventually only hear our minds telling us what we cannot do and how useless we are. This programming leads us to hear only the negatives instead of the positives. A negative mindset about ourselves stops us from using our unique talents and seeing our potential. Our inability to see our capabilities and skills hinders us from functioning as we should. We are disqualifying ourselves from helping others by not viewing ourselves correctly. By not performing as we should, we turn inwards instead of outwards and don't reach out to help others in need.

Our tendency to harbor negativity, fueled by our self-pity, inadvertently drives people away instead of drawing them closer to us. Pity, when unchecked, fosters the development of a victim mentality. Our victim mentality hinders our ability to connect with others meaningfully. The negative outlook and victim mentality we adopt act as a repellent, making it challenging to establish genuine relationships. This victim mentality often manifests in childish, controlling behavior, disrupting our capacity to relate to others as mature individuals. Striving for control stems from a desire for attention, even if it's negative, rather than no attention at all. Such behavior undermines relationships and impedes our ability to forge authentic connections. In a marital context, partners seek maturity and equality, not a partner who exhibits childlike behaviors and attempts to exert control.

Engaging in childish and controlling behavior prompts us to pout and employ silent defiance to garner negative attention. Because of our victim mentality and immature actions, we struggle to build close relationships, leading us to push people away. Our self-pity makes us work to recognize our uniqueness, abilities, and strengths. Our blindness to these results in stunted growth in those areas. Remaining in our negative victimization makes us continually feel like the underdog.

Dr. Bruce Thompson's book "Walls of My Heart" talks about three mentalities that people can allow to form within themselves. First, the top dog must always win by being first and the best at everything. Second, the underdog who sees ourselves as never being good enough or the underdog.[10]

We all find ourselves in one of these categories: individuals periodically grappling with challenges, particularly those tied to our sense of self-pity, often prefer to reside in the underdog state. Inhabiting this underdog state causes individuals facing rejection to overlook our strengths, uniqueness, and talents. Unfortunately, embracing this underdog mentality leads us to disregard the value we could provide to others even before attempting—our unwillingness to try hampers our capacity to grow and function as effectively as possible.

We become so focused on negativity that we can no longer see our worth, and we are not able or willing to function as we should. Our negativity and wrong focus cause us to be pessimistic, always seeing our glasses as half empty rather than half full. Instead of bringing others closer, our defeatist attitude pushes them away. Our cynical negativity leads to us becoming jealous and competitive. Negative emotions like jealousy and envy can make people doubt our unique qualities. Jealousy and competitiveness make us react badly, not wanting to receive help from others. We need to see others as helpers to improve our abilities. Seeing others' help as something negative leads us to become controlling. Being controlling is an issue that people find themselves constantly caught up in.

---

[10] Thompson, B. R. T., & Thompson, B. R. (1989). *Walls of my heart.*

BREAKTHROUGH

SHIFT IN FOCUS AND MATURE RELATIONSHIPS

Challenged individuals seeking liberation from misery often embark on a journey of positive change. This transformation involves redirecting focus toward others, abandoning childish behavior, and actively working to repair strained relationships. By fostering mature connections, individuals break free from self-pity and isolation.

ATTITUDE ADJUSTMENT AND DEVELOPMENT

Liberation from misery entails a fundamental shift in attitude and responses. Challenged individuals strive to cultivate a positive mindset, actively work on leveraging their strengths, and adopt respectful and considerate behaviors toward others. This intentional transformation builds a foundation for personal growth and improved interactions.

SELF-DISCOVERY AND POSITIVE OUTLOOK

Freedom from misery involves recognizing one's inherent value and strengths. Challenged individuals focus on embracing their uniqueness, fostering a positive outlook, and consciously avoiding the pitfalls of jealousy and competitiveness. This shift towards self-appreciation allows for a more fulfilling and contented life.

We break through self-pity challenges by focusing on others and how we can help or assist them rather than remaining stuck on our weaknesses or flaws. Helping others helps us break free from feeling stuck. We remember others would rather see us try to do something than have us do nothing. Faced with many individuals in desperate need, our primary concern should not be whether a helper executes tasks perfectly. Others would rather see us willing to show them kindness than hesitate because we don't think we can do it perfectly.

We should remain open and receptive to receiving guidance when they make mistakes, acknowledging that there is always room for improvement. Others must extend a helping hand instead of looking the other way. Recognizing that others need us allows us to break free from negative cycles and shift our focus from self-centered concerns to helping others. As challenged individuals overcome self-limitations and actively reach out to assist those around them, a sense of joy emerges. This shift allows us to appreciate our capabilities rather than dwelling on perceived limitations. By fostering a mindset of helping others and cultivating positivity, a transformation in attitude becomes possible. A positive outlook contributes to building strong relationships and paves the way for success. It motivates us to mend past relationships strained or broken by our previous self-pity mindset.

We can overcome self-pity by changing our attitudes toward ourselves and others. When we see things correctly, we stop feeling sorry for ourselves. Instead of focusing on our own needs or inadequacies, we respond to the needs of others around us. The more we respond to others' needs, the less we think about ourselves. By responding to others' needs, we can see how we are to function. The more we function, the more we can see what we have within ourselves to give to others in need. Through the joy we experience, as we help others, we overcome our emotional needs and lose our victim mentality. We find our victim mentality replaced by the joy of focusing on helping others with their needs. The longer we help others, the more we see our blindness replaced by a new passion for those in need. The more passionate we become, the greater our desire grows to help others, and we find out to see how we function best. A positive self-image comes from functioning well. Knowing our value and what we can offer affects our behavior towards others and ourselves. Seeing things through our fresh eyes allows us to learn valuable lessons as we help others and function as we should. Seeing things differently radically changes our perspective on life. We complained about walking with leg pain until we saw Nick Vujicic, who has no legs but is still joyful.[11]

We can overcome pity and change their attitude when they face a challenge. This change in perspective can help us move from a victim to a victor. Having a victor mentality moves us from pity to being able to overcome and encourage others. When I tell my story of growing up with cerebral palsy and being bullied, I talk about how my change of attitude about myself changed my life. I don't want people to feel sorry for me when telling my story. I want us to go away saying: "If Bradley could be so radically changed, I can change too."

As challenged people change their attitudes and outlook on life, it causes us to embrace our uniqueness, value, and

---

[11] Limbs, L. W. (2024, March 18). *Home - NickV Ministries*. NickV Ministries. https://nickvministries.org/

significance. I want to motivate us to turn our weaknesses into strengths. From my life journey, I've discovered that we are all like tea bags; our authentic flavor comes out when dropped into boiling water (hard times or challenges). The flavor shows us what is deep within us that may still need to be worked on. If it's good, if not, it shows what needs to be changed deep within.

As Dwight L. Moody said:
"Character is what you are in the dark."

Therefore, our darkest times show what flaws still need to be worked on and what character needs to be developed.

Those who face challenges can shift their perspective from negative to positive by seeing the glass as half full instead of half empty. When challenged people are optimistic, we let others celebrate us without pushing us away. As others celebrate us more, we become more confident about ourselves and what we offer. The security of our identity prevents us from comparing ourselves and continually trying to be the best. Our lack of comparison prevents us from becoming jealous.

Overcoming jealousy helps us not feel like we must always be the best at what we do. Free from competition and jealousy, we enjoy being ourselves and functioning as we should. As we work joyfully, others affirm and celebrate us instead of rejecting us. The less room others give us for pity, the more we feel affirmed and celebrated. Our lack of self-focus causes us to celebrate others as we should. Our celebration leads to honor and respect instead of breaking others down so we can look like the best.

INSPIRE

OUTREACH AND RELATIONSHIP RESTORATION

Challenged individuals, determined to break through the shackles of self-pity, take proactive steps to inspire others. This includes actively reaching out positively, ensuring they meet their needs, and actively working towards restoring broken relationships. By fostering a climate of understanding and connection, they set an example for others to do the same.

OVERCOMING VICTIM MENTALITY

Breaking free from a victim mentality is pivotal for challenged individuals seeking to inspire others. By recognizing and leveraging their strengths, they demonstrate resilience and self-empowerment. Showing honor even in the face of challenges becomes a powerful motivator for themselves and those around them.

OVERCOMERS WHO CELEBRATE POSITIVITY

Challenged individuals become beacons of inspiration by embracing the identity of overcomers. Valuing themselves and cultivating a positive mindset, they celebrate not only their victories but also the successes of others. This collective celebration encourages and motivates others to adopt a similar outlook on challenges.

We inspire others to care more about those in their community. Focusing on others instead of only on themselves inspires them to see the needs of others by looking beyond themselves. As they see others' needs, it inspires them not to be naval gazers. But to reach out to meet

155

the needs of those around them daily. As they meet other's needs, it inspires them to direct, inspire, motivate, and show sacrificial care as they reach out to meet the needs of others. When they meet the needs of those around them with the right heart and motivation, they are not controlling.

We inspire others not to gain pity from others but to meet their needs. When they let go of the need to control, they find inspiration in how others gravitate to them instead of being pushed away. As they no longer repel others through their pity, their relationships with them grow as they should. They develop these relationships instead of pushing others away through their negativity and control and wanting sympathy. Their lack of negativity and control causes their relationships to grow without using self-pity as a manipulative tool.

A positive attitude and focus inspire them to improve their relationships and see how positive relationships cause others to want to be with them instead of running away. Inspiring them to be selfless and help others by caring for and spending time with them. We inspire others to focus on their strengths, not their weaknesses. Focusing on their strengths releases them from the blindness of their pity. Focusing on their strengths inspires them to see how to help those in need. As they focus on the right thing, they get inspired by how others positively respond to their efforts. Others' positive responses to their help spur them on to do more. After being positively spurred on, they enjoy helping others. Their joy draws others to join them instead of their pity driving others away.

They no longer use pity as a manipulative tool, as they see people drawn to their joy instead of repelled by pity. Knowing pity can manipulate and control, so they inspire others through pleasure, not manipulation or control. Instead of being overbearing and pitiful, they experience the joy of reaching out to help others and inspire them to do the same. Through their happiness, they inspire others to see how powerful it is to become outwardly focused instead of pitiful. They inspire others by focusing on positivity instead of negativity, fueled by pity.

As long as I focused on my cerebral palsy, I restricted myself. However, things radically changed when I began focusing on how my sensitivities could help others. I found so much fulfillment in being a sensitive and caring person I didn't want to stop. The more I used my sensitivity to help others and saw its positive impact on them, the more I wanted to continue doing it. As they responded positively, it encouraged me I had no time for a pity party. Their support helped me continue speaking even if people needed help understanding me.

When they heard my sincerity, they reacted positively. When pity made me feel bad about speaking slowly, I would ignore it. However, when I began visiting other countries, the interpreters thanked me for talking slowly. What they said helped me to see the positive side of speaking slowly. Pity discourages rejected people from recognizing their strengths and focusing only on their weaknesses.

We inspire others to see the importance of looking at things from another viewpoint. By looking at things differently, they can develop the correct mindset. As they create the right way of thinking, they inspire others to see themselves as victors instead of victims. They see themselves as victors, enabling them to push through their hardships instead of despising them. Learning to push through as victors inspires them to know some of our greatest life lessons from their challenges. We inspire others to take the time needed to see what they can learn from their challenges. Changing how they see their struggles or challenges makes them feel excited about what they have learned instead of feeling sorry for themselves. By embracing their weaknesses instead of rejecting or despising them, they function as they should and help others.

David Ring is a man with cerebral palsy, and here is a quote I heard him say:

"When you eat with me, watch out for flying food, as I shake so much. Do I put my fork down and quit eating because I shake? No, why did you put your folks down and quit eating?" One of his most excellent punchlines is: *"I have cerebral palsy. What's your problem?"*[12]

As we overcome our pity, we inspire others to see themselves as overcomers who value who they are and what they can offer to others. Seeing themselves as valuable inspires them to function differently. They no longer allow pity to rob them or others of what they must give. Their new perspective of themselves and what they have to give inspires them to share more of themselves with them. The more they function as they should, the more they see how

---

[12] *HOME | davidring*. (n.d.). Davidring. https://www.davidring.org/

their abilities far outweigh their inabilities. Seeing the value of their weakness gives them tremendous courage and boldness to share what they have instead of being robbed by pity.

The bolder and more courageous they become, the greater joy they experience. Their happiness becomes so contagious that it affects others. They find joy in helping others renew their minds of their negative thoughts and pity and replace them with positive thoughts. I never thought I would become a teacher, as students mocked me for my slow speech. My negativity caused me not to want to get up and speak in front of people, yet that is what I began doing as a career, and I love it. Had I stayed focused on my pity with a 'woe-is-me' attitude, I would have robbed many of my teaching skills and ability.

We inspire others to see how much potential they have within themselves and to function as best they can. They see their lives as half-full instead of half-empty as they work as they should. Seeing they have something of value within them inspires others to look at themselves as valuable. Their ability to see their value inspires them to identify their unique function. As they function uniquely, others recognize them as we should. Being recognized allows them to feel as though they have worth. Feeling worthy and valuable inspires them to reach out and give as much as possible to others. Disabled individuals inspire others to explore their unique abilities and not let self-pity hinder them before trying to do what they need to do.

We inspire others to embrace their unique abilities instead of being held back by pity and motivate them to contribute to their unique skills without comparison. As they stop comparing themselves to others, they stop giving room to jealousy and envy, which leads to competition. Being inspired to enjoy being themselves, free of jealousy, envy, and competition. As they learn to be themselves, they no longer need to compete with others but complement them. They overcome their pity by inspiring others to complete and help those in need. Coming from a joyful heart, their submission to others enables them to honor and respect others instead of being jealous or envying them.

CONCLUSION

My radical change of focus to overcome the challenges of disdain and pity came when I accepted who I was and what I uniquely offered to others. My self-acceptance made me more sensitive to people's needs around me and able to see what I could do for us. It caused me to be more sensitive to our needs than my pity. Thanks to my newfound sensitivity, I broke free from the negative pity cycle I had been in for years. My freedom released me from being overly focused on what I couldn't do because of my handicap to being focused on how sensitive I was. My freedom from pity enabled me to go to places I never dreamed possible. I traveled to 38 countries, wrote a book, married, adopted children, and taught people about my experiences.

My life's journey inspired me to write this book. I desired to see people set free to fulfill what we must complete throughout our lives and boldly function in it. Had I remained in my prison of pity, I would not be writing what I am now to encourage you on your life's journey.

APPLICATION

1. What untapped potential is pity allowing you to rob others of receiving from you?

2. Please let go of the lies and embrace the truth that you have something unique no one else does.

3. What fingerprints will you leave on the lives of those around you who need what you have within you?

4. What attitudes can open the door to pity to get a hold of your life?

5. Why do you need to guard against jealousy and envy?

CHAPTER THIRTEEN
THE CHALLENGE OF DENIAL

"Why am I not telling others what I should be, and why am I suddenly in denial when people usually call me a teaching machine?" I asked myself these two questions on the third day of a personal growth seminar, where I'd remained as silent as possible for the first two days. I remained silent because I was unfamiliar with the group's leaders, except for the leaders running the course. My reaction surprised me as I had been so excited about doing the training course. Therefore, I dug deeper to find out why it was reacting in denial of what I offered instead of getting fully engaged.

My denial perplexed me as I felt I'd already overcome many rejection challenges and mastered most of them. However, as I dug deeper, I found the answers I was searching for, even though it was uncomfortable. I discovered a profound truth that would affect the rest of my life from then on. I held back my ideas in a group, especially with leaders, until I felt secure enough that they would accept me. When I realized what I had done, I later felt guilty for being so selfish. My guilt led to feelings of shame for selfishly withholding my treasures from those who could have benefitted from them if I had shared them.

BREAKDOWN

SELF-DENIAL AND WITHDRAWAL

Challenged individuals grappling with the negative consequences of self-denial, selfishness, and shame often withdraw from fulfilling their potential contributions. This withdrawal prevents them from engaging in meaningful actions and sharing their abilities, ultimately limiting their impact on others.

SHYNESS AND LACK OF SELF-APPRECIATION

Challenged individuals may adopt a façade of shyness in response to internal struggles, downplaying their capabilities. This self-deprecating attitude hinders genuine appreciation for their offerings, as they perceive others as superior. This self-perceived inferiority becomes a barrier to openly sharing their strengths with those around them.

PORTRAY PITY-DRIVEN SELFISHNESS

Some individuals project a false image of themselves to cope with challenges. This false portrayal, often fueled by a desire for pity, can lead to a cycle of selfishness and shame. In projecting an inaccurate image, individuals may inadvertently isolate themselves and miss opportunities for authentic relationships with others.

People with difficulties may struggle to reveal their hidden skills and talents to others because of inner conflicts and barriers. Our self-denial blocks us from interacting with others as we should, boldly and confidently. Our struggle to be confident or bold causes us to withdraw from people, especially unfamiliar ones. We become even more withdrawn when in group settings with strangers. Therefore, we grow more cautious when we find ourselves in an unknown group. Our caution leads us to develop a pattern of choosing only to be open to give what we have until we feel secure enough to do so. Once we feel confident enough, we hesitantly start reaching out to provide something to the group.

Hesitation often holds us back from getting engaged and involved as we ought to, which keeps us back. We fear, challenge, and hesitate to engage. Our lack of engagement and involvement, driven by fear, leads to self-loathing. All these opposing challenges make us feel more secure in our rejection than in getting engaged and involved as we should. Being blinded by our opposing challenges, we do not open up and share our treasures and uniqueness with others. When we see how selfish we've been, we regret it, knowing that we may have denied others what we can give freely and uniquely.

We often conceal our inherent selfishness and self-denial by projecting an image of having nothing to offer to others. This facade creates a barrier between us and others, impeding positive engagement. The masks we wear can give the impression of introversion and shyness, making it challenging for others to extend help. Our false image may lead others to believe we are not open to building meaningful relationships. Our masks and misleading portrayals might deceive others into thinking we have little to contribute. Unfortunately, our self-perceived shyness hinders others from truly understanding who we are, masking genuine humility with a facade.

The false humility, rooted in fear and self-denial, prevents us from embodying the boldness and confidence we should embrace. Succumbing to our fears and self-denial devalues our self-worth, impacting self-esteem and making us susceptible to the pitfalls of the pity challenge once more. Believing the falsehood that we possess little or nothing to offer others disqualifies us in our own eyes. Self-disqualification leads us to view others as more valuable, resulting in our silence while others speak, further disqualifying ourselves in a cycle of negative self-perception.

We may hide our true worth and abilities, pretending to have nothing to offer. While making people think we are of little value, we deceptively and selfishly portray a false image of ourselves. Therefore, we do not ask others for their input or help, leading to feelings of exclusion. Our feelings of being excluded make us battle again with the challenge of pity, which we addressed in our previous chapter. We lack self-confidence because of our self-denial, which allows pity to take over again. These three then cause us to adopt a victim mentality once again.

Our woe-is-me mentality causes us to think:

"Why didn't they allow me to share what I had to contribute? Our fear-driven selfishness prevents us from engaging with others.

BREAKTHROUGH

TRANSPARENCY AND FUNCTIONALITY

Individuals aspiring to overcome challenges confront obstacles when self-denial, fear, and pity hold sway. Overcoming these barriers involves a decisive shift. This means no longer withdrawing. They make a breakthrough by openly sharing their struggles and functioning. This transparency enables them to receive support and foster a climate of understanding.

AUTHENTICITY AND SELF-APPRECIATION

To navigate challenges successfully, individuals discard pretenses and cultivate an authentic self-image. They actively appreciate and acknowledge their capabilities, recognizing the value they bring to the table. This shift in mindset enables a more positive and empowered approach to overcoming obstacles.

ACCURATE SELF-PORTRAYAL AND RESILIENCE

Overcoming challenges requires individuals to represent themselves and their capabilities accurately. Rejecting the temptation to feed on pity and refusing to be driven by fear, they showcase their strengths realistically. This authentic self-portrayal is a foundation for resilience, enabling them to tackle challenges head-on with confidence and determination.

Overcoming challenges involves accepting the truth about one's actions and reactions. We face rejection but still engage with others to overcome self-denial, fear, and pity. Helping others without being stopped by our self-doubt, fear, or pity. As we get engaged, we give our best instead of selfishly withholding our unique abilities. We serve with our whole heart and soul, using all our unique abilities to assist in any way possible. We become mindful as we help with how much we need others to help us see ourself-denial, fear, and pity. Our changed perspective helps us become filled with compassion for others instead of self-denial, fear, and pity. I realized my selfishness after questioning myself and seeking help from others. Being open and honest about challenges like self-denial, fear, and pity can help people overcome and achieve goals. Gaining ongoing breakthroughs is not a quick fix; it requires time and patience. Having the right guide and being willing to recognize these challenges speed up the process radically.

I conquered the obstacles within myself by transcending self-denial, fear, and self-pity, gaining a profound understanding of my internal struggles. This positive decision began a transformative journey that spanned fourteen years. Recognizing the impact of my self-denial, fear, and pity on my self-confidence was initially shocking. Still, it prompted me to change and fully engage in a life-altering seminar. The revelation of my selfishness hidden beneath false humility brought about a fundamental shift in my mindset. This transformation proved instrumental, laying the foundation for writing the book I present today. Through this process, I became more assertive and eager to share what I have with anyone willing to receive it. I developed the ability to speak confidently without being overly affected by others' responses, signifying personal growth and empowerment.

My newfound boldness caused me to no longer be introverted and shy when I was in a group. My courage caused me to think: "What do I have to give these people from my treasure chest, and how can I best help us?" Seeing my needs allowed me to use my previously rejected sensitivity as something positive, not negative. I looked more to see how I could help us instead of withdrawing in fear of how we may reject what I gave us. My new perspective motivated me to be bold and confident in functioning as I should, free from self-denial, fear, and pity. The more I gave myself, the more needs motivated me to give more. Giving more helps those in need to tap into our hidden resources, which we use to function better.

My encouragement filled me with joy, replacing my self-denial, fear, and pity with a desire to give as much as possible. The more I gave myself, the less I retreated into self-denial, fear, and pity. Instead of fleeing, I advanced, feeling like I had value and something worth giving. Seeing what I had was of value and worth. This motivated me to give with all my heart and soul. I recognized that what I had to provide us with was unique to me and that I functioned differently.

Functioning in my uniqueness and using my abilities to help those in need prevented me from selfishly robbing others of what I had to give. As I pushed past my self-denial, fear, and self-pity, I helped others not to fall into the same traps I did. I could show others how to recognize and avoid those traps or challenges. By identifying and knowing how to overcome our pitfalls or challenges, I could help others not to suffer as I did. I empowered people to do the same by telling us how I overcame my traps, challenges, and life lessons. We entrust ourselves to help others and recognize our strengths by embracing what I taught.

We overcome self-doubt by recognizing our worth and abilities. By letting go of our masks and pretending to have nothing, we push through our self-denial, fear, and self-pity and start functioning as we should. As we work correctly, we do so with all our heart and soul and cease being people-pleasers. Instead of being people-pleasers, we become life-giving helpers who are sensitive to the needs of others. Seeing the needs of others inspires us to recognize our unique ability to provide help by addressing those needs.

We overcome self-denial, fear, and self-pity to make a difference for those in need. We give others what we have with all our hearts and souls without being concerned about their rejection. As we entirely give ourselves to others' needs, we become filled with joy that spurs us to provide even more of ourselves. Our joy breaks our old negative cycle of self-denial, fear, pity, and a victim mentality and replaces the negative with the positive. Our joy and positivity inspire us to give ourselves selflessly even more to help others in need, increasing our joy. Finding joy in serving others in need replaces our self-denial, fear, and pity that we no longer battle with it. We find joy in serving and being ourselves, which makes us let go of negative emotions.

INSPIRE

BRAVERY AND EMBRACING UNIQUENESS

Challenged individuals overcome self-doubt, fear, and self-pity, serving as beacons of inspiration for others.

They inspire bravery in new social situations by boldly embracing their unique capabilities. Recognizing individual strengths fosters confidence, enabling them to help those in need without fear of rejection.

COLLABORATION TO BREAK DOWN WALLS

Acknowledging their unique abilities, challenged individuals understand the power of collaboration. They recognize that helping others and working together can be more effective than tackling challenges alone. This realization prompts them to break down selfish walls, paving the way for a culture of caring and sharing among our friends and colleagues.

CARE OVER PERFECTION AND FEAR

Challenged individuals shift their focus from perfection and fear of rejection to the power of caring and sharing. The care they extend pushes them past self-denial, fear, and pity, motivating them to do their best for those in need. By prioritizing the needs of others over their concerns, they foster positive interactions and create a supportive environment.

FREEDOM FROM REGRET

Helping others becomes a liberating force, freeing individuals from regret and the feeling of not giving enough. Recognizing the significance of reaching out in need challenges individuals to interact positively with others. This creates a cycle of support and understanding that benefits themselves and their community.

Helping others brings joy and motivates shy people to become confident and optimistic. As we reach outward to help as we should, we engage with others instead of feeling intimidated by them. Becoming engaged with them inspires them and helps them overcome their self-worth challenge. Correctly recognizing them for their genuine, caring help helps them feel fulfilled in what they have achieved.

The positive response from others inspires them to know that their contributions matter and make a difference. Recognizing their contributions gives them a sense of value that spurs them to sacrifice more of themselves. They can gain greater insight into their unique gifts by aiding others more. They recognize that others suffer loss if they do not offer what they uniquely can offer. Seeing how significant others' needs inspires them to let go of their needs to help others instead. Assisting others and valuing their uniqueness inspires them to overcome self-denial, fear, and self-pity. I desired to change as I saw what I was doing through my self-denial, fear, and pity, which caused me not to engage in the seminar fully. My desire for change was so deep it began breaking a pattern I'd developed over the years. My decision that day made my interactions with people better, especially with leaders and strangers.

We inspire others to be themselves without fear of judgment from strangers. Choosing to make mistakes instead of denying others their unique help. Allowing them to push past their self-denial, fear, and self-pity. Instead of fearing making mistakes, they value the life lessons learned through them. Humbly admitting their mistakes and growing through them instead of rejecting them. Embracing their weaknesses and mistakes rather than dismissing or despising them gives them more to contribute to others. Being inspired to focus on their uniqueness and to do their best keeps them moving forward positively. Being inspired to face their fears, accept themselves, and move forward positively, knowing they cannot control how others react to them. Not letting others control them and focusing on doing what they want to force them to do. They value their uniqueness and are inspired to help others without worrying about their reaction. By helping others instead of focusing on themselves, they break free of their fear-driven victim mentality.

CONCLUSION

I learned my lesson at the seminar and began sharing with others instead of holding back. I got fully engaged during the remaining time that the leaders commented on it. They motivated me to see the benefits of collaborating instead of keeping things to myself. If you don't contribute what you have, it may rob others of your unique contribution, and you'll regret it. However, if you offer your best to others, you will experience a sense of fulfillment and relief and won't feel guilt, shame, or regret.

OVERCOMING REJECTION

APPLICATION

1. Are you willing to let go of your fear and allow yourself to take risks, giving boldly what you can to those around you?

2. What fears make you hold back your contribution from others?

3. What mindsets may you have to change?

4. What happens when you hold back from giving others what you should?

5. What emotions do you feel when you have given what you should have to others?

CHAPTER FOURTEEN
THE CHALLENGE OF
BEING REPRESSED

"How will they react when I speak slowly because of my cerebral palsy? How will I react if they laugh or make fun of me?" These questions flooded my mind as I was about to go on stage to address a group of people I would offer to come and teach in the coming year. Instead of looking back at what I'd achieved in the past, my repression of myself was trying to get me to disqualify myself before I began or tried. This was a challenge I often faced whenever I was about to break new ground and move into teaching a new group. This challenge would lie to me and bring up my past mistakes or negative reactions of others to stop me from succeeding.

BREAKDOWN

EMOTIONAL REPRESSION AND INSECURITY

Challenged individuals grappling with the struggle to repress their emotions often find themselves burdened by feelings of insecurity and shyness. The internal conflict between expressing and suppressing emotions can create a barrier to self-confidence and open interaction with others.

REFRAINING FROM SELF-ISOLATION

The decision to refrain from speaking, driven by the challenges of emotional repression, may inadvertently lead to self-isolation. Fears of judgment or rejection can hinder individuals from expressing themselves when they should, contributing to a sense of detachment from social interactions.

SILENCE, JUDGMENT, AND CRITICISM

Some individuals may remain silent in the face of emotional struggles, adopting a stance of judgment or criticism toward those who speak boldly. This defensive response can be a coping mechanism but also perpetuates a cycle of negative emotions and strained social dynamics.

By focusing too much on ourselves, we listen more to the lies about ourselves than the truth. We go through many of the same challenges we did in battling self-pity. Listening to the lies instead of stopping them as soon as they start gives them a foothold in our minds. The longer the foothold may grow in our minds, the easier it is for them to get into our hearts. By believing these lies and giving them a foothold in our minds and hearts, we allow them to grow even stronger within us. Eventually, we allow these lies to deceive us and find it hard to know what is true. We need to be more transparent about the truth about ourselves as we struggle to overcome this challenge of being repressed.

We need truthful friends to help us distinguish between truth and lies and avoid being trapped in lies for too long. The lies fill us so that they rob us of our self-confidence. We need more confidence and can't function as we should around others. Listening to lies and letting wrong thoughts grow within us hinders us from working boldly. We also say, "Am I not good enough to do that?" "What if they realize I am still learning and don't have the necessary answers?" "What if I say the wrong thing and make a fool of myself?"

THE CHALLENGE OF BEING REPRESSED

Repression fills our minds with these negative thoughts so much that we quit before trying. Our negative thoughts cause us to rob others of what we have to give them. The negativity created by repression directly affects our willpower and motivation to function. Negative thoughts can lead to fear, doubt, and unbelief, causing paralysis.

When grappling with repression, we often find comfort in sticking to familiar circles. This tendency to remain within the known confines limits our ability to reach out and assist those unfamiliar with it. Our reluctance to step into the unknown hinders us from taking risks and expanding our capacity to help others. Rather than venturing into the unfamiliar, we mistakenly place a false sense of security in the comfort of the familiar. This inclination to stay within our comfort zone restricts our ability to function outside the bounds of familiarity, impeding personal growth and development.

Choosing false comfort over growth prevents us from experiencing the stretching and expansion needed to realize our full potential. Our unwillingness to grow and develop stunts our progress and denies others the opportunity to benefit from the unique insights they could acquire. Fear of taking risks and resisting the stretching process hampers us from reaching our full potential, fostering a sense of incompetence and a perceived need for more to offer others. This feeling of inadequacy intensifies repression as our fears perpetuate a self-image of shyness. In projecting this false image, we inadvertently misrepresent ourselves and diminish the value we could bring to others.

OVERCOMING REJECTION

While being deceived by fear, timidity, and shyness, we allow a negative false cycle to develop within ourselves. The incorrect negative process we buy into through our repression hinders us from interacting with others as we should. We need help forming strong bonds with others, which hinders our ability to work well together. Our lack of relationships with those who could help us function best directly affects our confidence and ability. Lacking the confidence needed, we choose only to work as we should with those we are comfortable with. This challenge of feeling repressed caused me to fear getting up to speak in front of the people I was to be teaching. My repression also caused me to portray a false image of myself when I was in a group of people, I was not familiar with. Rejected people will not function as they should because of repression until they feel comfortable that they will not be rejected.

When battling repression, we seek safety in solitude. However, in our place of solitude, we allow the lies to attack our minds until we become tormented by them. Our minds become so filled with lies that they prevent us from functioning. If we do not have others helping us, soon enough, we will sink deeper and deeper into our negativity and self-disqualification. Eventually, we become so negative we can see nothing else but how little we can do. Unable to see our full potential, we allow negative thoughts to take over our minds. Our blindness and negative thoughts then can gain such strength that they become a twister of enormous power.

Later, learning that tormenting twisters are much more challenging to overcome than the average storms we encounter. If we can't address our problems quickly enough, we get overwhelmed by the situation. Repression can cause damage that needs to be cleaned up, like a tornado that separates people who need help. The same is true with the challenging twisters of repression. Repression twisters leave rejected people stuck in a place of isolation. When isolated, we give up on ourselves and lose our passion to function as we should. A lack of desire deceives us into thinking we have nothing to contribute to others in need. Our deception further closes our eyes to our abilities and capabilities and deprives those around us of what we should give them. We deprive both ourselves and those in need.

People who feel repressed may isolate themselves instead of interacting with others. They become hurt by remaining defiant instead of reaching out to build new, lasting friendships. Often, we remain defiant because we are judgmental of certain people we have had negative experiences with. Being judgmental causes us to become overly focused on what others may think of us or how they may judge us. Our judgmental attitude hinders us from reaching out to others as we should. Instead of reaching out and being open about our feelings, we repress ourselves as we judge others unfairly.

Our response of being judgmental towards others makes us selfishly choose to withdraw. Through our withdrawal, we end up not opening up as we should to others, especially those we are unfamiliar with. Being judgmental leads to a negative tendency to become critical of ourselves and others. This criticism hinders us from reaching out as we should to others working with us. Our selfish isolation results in us not growing or allowing ourselves to be stretched to reach our full potential. A lack of willingness to let others help us hinders our personal growth and character development.

BREAKTHROUGH

BUILDING RELATIONSHIPS AND RESOURCES

Those who understand the challenges others face should take the initiative to mend relationships and make amends. This involves actively building connections, providing necessary resources, and getting involved in the lives of those affected. Individuals contribute to the healing process by taking these steps and creating a supportive environment.

COURAGEOUS FUNCTIONING

Acknowledging challenges is just the first step; individuals must decide to share their uniqueness with others. This choice entails overcoming negative emotions that may hold them back. By courageously functioning as they should, individuals demonstrate resilience and a commitment to move beyond the constraints of emotional struggles.

LETTING GO OF JUDGMENT

To honestly share their uniqueness, individuals must let go of judgmental attitudes and allow others to discover who they are. This involves fostering an environment of acceptance and understanding. Doing so creates space for authentic connections, enabling others to see beyond challenges and appreciate the individual for their true self.

THE CHALLENGE OF BEING REPRESSED

We reach out and build new relationships to break through repression. We reach out instead of listening to the disqualifying lies in our minds and hearts. When we reach out, we do not limit it to simply the ones we are familiar with and comfortable around. Instead, we go beyond our comfort zones and choose to open up and engage with new people we are not familiar with and who don't know us. We choose to interact with new people, believing in our abilities and not concerned about how others will react. Our confidence strengthens our ability to function and help others.

As we help others, we know that not everyone will receive what we have to give us. Understanding that not all will be receptive to us frees us from wrong expectations and lies. We place our confidence more in the truth of who we are and how we are to function than in the lies of repression. Putting our faith in the truth stops us from listening to repressions and lies. Being truthful helps us communicate better with everyone, even unfamiliar people. Having the right communication tools prepares us to function with total confidence. Our confidence results in us becoming more productive in the way we work.

As we confidently embrace our identity and understand our intended function, we break free from fear and self-repression. This newfound freedom empowers us to take risks and boldly step into the roles we are meant to fulfill. In my case, despite having been teaching for almost twenty-five years, encouragement from my board prompted me to refine my communication skills further.

Responding to this encouragement, I sought out a training course and found one called 'Advance Your Reach.'

The course provided valuable instruction on presenting messages effectively, with a practical workshop culminating in a presentation to a large group. Notably, I was chosen from my group of ten to contribute to the gathering of two hundred and eighty and later selected as one of the seven finalists in the course's speak-off. The experience marked a turning point, significantly boosting my confidence in presentations.

The positive changes in my approach were noticeable, garnering feedback from both board members and peers. The affirming responses to my teaching, using the tools acquired from the training, further fueled my motivation to continue improving. The training enhanced my skills and inspired me to embrace a bolder approach, a transformation others acknowledged and appreciated.

People who desire to overcome self-repression need to be more outspoken. I became more outspoken after recognizing my habit of not getting involved with strangers, which I discovered during a training course I attended in 1996. Despite my fear of rejection, I pushed past my fears and began interacting with people I never knew. On the third day, I got deeply engaged. It changed the next two days for me and was life-changing. I will always remember the profound lessons I learned. However, after doing the 'Advance Your Reach' course, my boldness went to an even greater level.

I learned to make deliberate choices when interacting with people, even if I didn't know them. I let go of my hypersensitivity, which had developed because I was mocked for my slow speech and movements while speaking.

I had to learn not to take things personally. The same applies to people trying to overcome rejection challenges.

Finding proper security requires understanding that our identity is rooted in who we are rather than solely in how we function or assist others. This perspective was directly addressed when we examined the performance challenges outlined in our first section. To reduce reliance on a functional identity, individuals with heightened sensitivity must recognize and acknowledge its detrimental effects on our well-being.

We gain the courage to speak the truth when we break through self-repression. As we speak the truth more boldly and function as we should, we become excited about how we are to work. Our excitement outweighs our fear and self-repression until we no longer want to hold back. Our excitement releases us from holding back what we uniquely have to give to others. It also leads to a positive sense of accomplishment that we want to help more and not keep what we have to ourselves. The more we give to others, the greater we benefit from each other's efforts and enthusiasm. Our enthusiasm is contagious and beneficial to both, giving us fulfillment in purpose and function.

Our mutual enthusiasm prevents what we have from being bottled up so long that it eventually explodes. If we keep it bottled up for too long, it can explode, causing the same adverse reaction as defiance. When we did not say what we should have, we exploded and controlled our relationships through our silent defiance.

When we withhold our talents, others inevitably seek those abilities elsewhere. This results in others being deprived of the opportunity to receive what we have to give them. Before overcoming the challenges of repression, I often experienced regret, witnessing others offer what I knew I should have. This regret motivated me to ensure that I contribute what I have to offer without allowing myself to be sidelined.

A similar experience holds for rejected individuals; the pain of witnessing missed opportunities often serves as a powerful catalyst. It compels them to resist allowing such instances to happen again. This realization drives a renewed determination not to let valuable contributions go unshared.

We break self-repression when we stop judging others before getting to know them. Taking the time to get to know them first helps us avoid the pain. Even if they remind us of someone who hurt us. We ask ourselves hard questions before judging them. We wonder who or what from our past has hurt us and caused us to overreact to similar people. Our adverse reaction shows us the need to look back and deal with the situation by choosing to release the person. Coping with it allows us to work through the pain instead of trying to hide it and pretend it did not affect us when it did. However, as we saw with the pity challenge, we do not continue to dwell on issues that have already been resolved and avoid becoming too introspective. The only reason to address a past issue is if it is triggering negative emotions within.

If we do not deal with past hurtful rejections or other matters, it is like refusing to remove the stinger after a bee has stung us. It will not simply disappear if we ignore it—it will fester and worsen. However, a stinger must only be removed correctly once, and then we must move on. Not addressing past or present relationship issues can negatively affect future relationships. Dealing with past or present problems and challenges prevents us from being overly judgmental. By being less critical, we learn not to judge a book by its cover but to get to know the person first. Understanding the person requires us to develop our relational skills and be humble enough to work through issues.

To conquer self-repression, we can seek support and guidance from others. Being humble enough to admit we need help is the first step we have to take. Then, we reach out to the right people to help or advise us. Others' helpful advice enables us to reach out more freely and frequently to people we have held back from previously. Reaching out to those we were fearful of or who we'd wrongly judged is also humbling. It empowered us to interact boldly and non-judgmentally because of our humility. The more we interact with each other, the more fulfilling and enjoyable it becomes. The cheerful pattern replaces the old, selfish one as we keep joyfully fulfilling it.

Our new positive habit makes us happy and improves our relationships. The new meaningful relationships help us see our past mistakes in a positive, different light. We no longer see our past mistakes as stumbling blocks to hold us back. Instead, we see them as life lessons we had to walk through to learn. Recognizing our challenges can give us and others valuable tools for future growth. They see us as building blocks that remove the tormenting, paralyzing fear of us. The torment is now replaced by inspiration that spurs us on to help others. Helping others inspires confidence and replaces self-repression. We feel encouraged by witnessing how stumbling blocks can positively affect us. Our encouragement helps them make progress. We act boldly and look for who we can help next.

INSPIRE

FUNCTIONING AND BUILDING RELATIONSHIPS

Challenged individuals serve as sources of inspiration by overcoming self-repression and functioning as they should. This involves actively reaching out to new people, extending a hand in building connections, and actively working to strengthen existing relationships. By doing so, they set an example of functional engagement that inspires those around them.

BOLDNESS WITHOUT WITHDRAWAL

Overcoming self-repression requires a bold and selfless approach to life. Challenged individuals inspire others by demonstrating these qualities without withdrawing from social interactions. They engage authentically, showcasing resilience and a commitment to personal growth despite facing challenges.

BUILDING NON-JUDGMENTAL RELATIONSHIPS

Challenged individuals inspire those around them by conquering fears and establishing non-judgmental relationships. They demonstrate the transformative power of embracing openness and acceptance by building connections with new people without succumbing to apprehensions. This overcoming mindset catalyzes positive change in both individuals and the community.

As others observe our breakthroughs and joy at no longer being repressed, it inspires them by overcoming our shyness and making new friends outside their usual group. Forming these relationships inspires others to function boldly as they should, helping others in any way possible. The more they engage and help others, the easier for them to work together. They conquer their fears of helping new people and see the positive response. As they overcome their fears and self-repression, joy replaces their fears and lies. Their joy and sense of fulfillment replace their self-doubt with confidence, creating a positive pattern. The new positive way they made brings them joy. This inspires them to help unfamiliar people in need.

Positive responses serve as encouragement, motivating them to cultivate their skills and extend assistance to others. Their enthusiasm becomes a powerful force, rendering them less susceptible to falsehoods. While there may be a fear of the unknown, their enthusiasm propels them to overcome it. This enthusiasm drives the development of new friendships and relationships with unfamiliar individuals, simultaneously strengthening their existing connections.

We inspire others to boldly break through their fears of opening up and functioning as they should. Encouraging them to leave their comfort zones and help unfamiliar people. As they reach out to new people, they push past their comfort zones and grow and function even more than they did. The more they grow and work correctly, the more they get to know others free of self-repression. The joy of seeing unfamiliar people and others being supported by them inspires them to reach out to more. They find joy in functioning as they should, giving them such a strong sense of fulfillment that they leave no room for self-repression.

Feeling fulfilled and joyful helps them and others function better and see through lies that try to hold them back. By listening to their joy-filled hearts instead of repression, they work best and give their all to what they do. Their joy in seeing what they can uniquely help others with replaces their hypersensitivity. Hypersensitivity is a challenge we will discuss in-depth in our final chapters. They become more mature and determined when they get over their hypersensitivity.

Overcoming repression helps them feel less alone and isolated. Instead of choosing to isolate themselves, they reach out and help others. Choosing to help others enables them to get to know each other and develop friendships. By making friends and meeting new people, they overcome their self-isolation. Their new friendships comfort them, seeing their isolating walls being demolished through these friendships. They feel stronger and break free from selfishness and self-pity by constantly reaching out to make friends. Free from their selfish pity, they focus outward to help others instead of turning inward to give pity a foothold. Their outward focus on wanting to help others helps them in their time of need instead of simply looking inwardly at their own needs. They prioritize others' needs over their own, which has positive results. The rewards of helping others and seeing them encouraged and inspired help them want to reach out more with their abilities.

The rewards of helping others build up their confidence so much that they do not want to stop helping them. As the momentum grows, they seek new people to help instead of letting their repression lead them into a lonely place of isolation.

Their joy and sense of fulfillment lead them to become loyal friends, not simply colleagues. Their loyalty helps and inspires others to become loyal to them, allowing a positive cycle of loyalty to be developed and nurtured. The longer they are dedicated, the stronger their friendships become, bringing joy and healing to all. The joy brings healing from fears caused by past hurts. Their joy-filled sense of fulfillment leads them to strive to find how they can function best to help those in need around them.

With the help of others, they hone their skills and abilities, using them to help others. They look for better ways to help and share their resources when they see positive results, to make a lasting impact, and to be more effective. They look primarily at how to grow their communication skills, as communication is critical to lasting friendships. Seeking help to hone their skills and communicate better is humbling, as it shows that they are just as needy as the ones they want to help. They show humility by expressing their needs instead of repressing them in pride. By being honest about their abilities, they open themselves to being vulnerable to others. Their humility breaks the cycle of isolation, loneliness, fear, pride, and judgment.

CONCLUSION

After years of struggle, a mentor helped me to understand my purpose and gain self-confidence. He encouraged me to recognize my abilities rather than being defined by my teaching role. Instead of repressing how I functioned, he helped me work on it correctly, knowing that teaching was what I did, but it was not who I was. He helped me let go of self-pity and focus on my teaching abilities to help others.

APPLICATION

1. How do you feel being in a group of people you don't know?

2. What voices can you direct your actions when those feelings arise?

3. Do those negative voices restrict you?

4. How are you allowing what you do to define who you are?

5. How do you see humility being a vital key to overcoming self-repression?

CHAPTER FIFTEEN
THE CHALLENGE OF BEING
OVERLY SELF-CONSCIOUS

"The leadership team has asked me to talk to you about not counseling people because of your cerebral palsy. The leadership team is concerned about how people battle to understand you because of your cerebral palsy."

This is what a colleague came and told me after I had recently chosen to go forward and help people. The challenge of pity and other challenges I have already addressed wanted to disqualify me and make me so self-conscious that I would give up and quit. However, as I mentioned in our introduction, one thing about people who have a handicap is we don't give up or leave quickly. However, I would have quit had it not been for my father coming alongside me and encouraging me not to give up. My father's encouragement made me more confident. So, I talked to my leaders and cleared up the misunderstanding. We worked through the misunderstanding, and I continued doing what I enjoyed: helping others in need.

BREAKDOWN

SEE PAST FAILURES AS ROADBLOCKS

Individuals grappling with self-consciousness often find themselves hindered by the weight of past failures. The tendency to focus on mistakes prevents them from embracing opportunities for growth and learning. The obsession with past errors becomes a barrier to progress, as it hampers the enthusiasm needed to progress and improve.

DECEPTIVE SELF-IMAGE

Excessive self-consciousness can lead to the creation of a deceptive self-image, especially in social and professional settings. The fear of judgment may prompt individuals to portray a false version of themselves, hindering their ability to be bold and authentic. This lack of boldness can be misconstrued as introversion, shyness, or an inability to express oneself, contributing to a cycle of negative self-perception.

DETRIMENTAL IMPACT ON ENGAGEMENT

The internalization of doubt and unbelief, fueled by self-consciousness, can drown out positive voices that encourage and motivate. This lack of confidence hampers engagement with others, as individuals may withhold their true selves, fearing rejection. By projecting a false image and failing to engage authentically, they unintentionally deter others and limit the sharing of their valuable contributions and talents.

When trapped in being overly conscious, we need the right people to give us a wake-up call. When others are bold enough to provide us with a wake-up call, it enables us to realize what we allow to happen. Their wake-up call helps us see what lies are deceiving us into thinking we have nothing of value to give or help others with. Something directly linked this challenge to our challenge of disdain, which we started this section with. Our disdain leads to us feeling that our life has no value, worth, or meaning. We are so self-conscious and negative that we don't see our unique abilities. Not being able to recognize our unique self-worth restricts us from helping others.

Caught in this challenge of being overly conscious, we feel worthless and dismiss our message, discrediting our uniqueness. We become so consumed by feelings of worthlessness that we only see the negative. A wrong focus prevents us from seeing our life message and how valuable we could be to others. We eventually become depressed and feel worthless because of our negative thoughts. We let negative lies close our eyes to our full potential and focus on our inadequacies. Negative feelings and inadequacies, fueled by fear, prevent us from trying to do what we should be doing. Our negative motivation, driven by fear, keeps saying, *"What if you do it wrong and make a mistake?"*

Our negative reasoning makes us focus more on past mistakes than present victories or potential. By listening to the wrong voices, instead of gaining momentum, we stay focused on our mistakes. Rather than using our unique abilities to help others, we let our past mistakes hold us back. Our strong focus makes us see our past failures as stumbling blocks that hold us back from doing what we should do to help others. Our strong focus causes us to ignore our stumbling blocks instead of seeing them as potential building blocks. Negativity closes our eyes to the potential we have for turning lemons into lemonade. We can't identify our challenges, which hinders our ability to move forward and positively impact others.

We need bold and courageous people to help challenge us, or we'll become more depressed and hopeless. We must recognize what is happening and reach out for help quickly to avoid being trapped in the wrong mindset. The longer we remain deceived, blinded, and trapped, the stronger our negative attitude becomes. Our negative mindset then says, *"You can never change. It's hopeless."*

This goes back to the challenge of negative self-talk we addressed in an earlier chapter. We don't let our past failures stop us, even when comparing ourselves to those who seem to have it all together. Doing so leads to us never taking a risk or trying to give what we have to offer, which is very selfish, as we rob others. Despite others investing in us, we feel guilty or ashamed for not using or sharing what we have learned. Challenged people often battle shame, which can be as powerful as fear.

BREAKTHROUGH

STRATEGIC PROGRESSION

Individuals facing challenges triumph over self-consciousness by adopting a strategic approach to move forward instead of retreating. This involves consciously navigating obstacles, embracing growth opportunities, and actively seeking positive strategies to break free from negative patterns.

FUNCTIONAL RESILIENCE

Overcoming self-consciousness requires pressing past failures and mistakes by continuing to function as intended. This resilience involves using challenges as opportunities to learn and grow rather than allowing them to become roadblocks. By functioning optimally despite setbacks, individuals can break free from self-doubt.

COURAGEOUS CONTRIBUTION

A key aspect of overcoming self-consciousness is choosing to help others courageously by giving of oneself. This involves using personal passions and experiences to initiate positive cycles of functioning. By sharing life lessons from overcoming challenges, individuals can guide others away from potential pitfalls, creating a supportive community that fosters growth and resilience.

We can escape being controlled, intimidated, or manipulated by others. By expressing ourselves boldly, overcoming our negative doubts, and showing others what we can offer. We move forward, valuing our life message and what we can offer others. Growing in boldness, we find help to excel in our areas of expertise. Doing this allows us to hone our unique skills and become more productive and creative instead of stuck in our old ways.

Our newfound creative productivity brings joy and stops our negative self-talk. This joy prevents us from making excuses and competing, allowing us to avoid jealousy and envy. Knowledge of our strengths will enable us to take risks without fear. Risk-taking brings joy and frees us from guilt for not helping others enough.

INSPIRE

FORWARD MOMENTUM OVER RETREAT

Challenged individuals initiate positive breakthroughs by moving forward instead of retreating in the face of difficulties. This deliberate decision involves resisting the urge to succumb to fear and self-consciousness, making positive choices that propel them towards personal growth and the opportunity to help others.

FUNCTIONAL EMPOWERMENT

Overcoming challenges entails functioning as one should, pressing past failures or mistakes to aid others. By leveraging personal experiences, individuals can transform setbacks into opportunities for learning and growth. This functional empowerment not only helps them overcome self-consciousness but also positions them to make meaningful contributions to the well-being of others.

COURAGEOUS OUTREACH

The journey of overcoming self-consciousness involves courageously reaching out to help others with one's resources and experiences. By extending a helping hand, individuals create a positive ripple effect, inspiring others to overcome their challenges. This courageous outreach fosters a sense of community and encourages the development of joyful giving patterns, replacing selfish and fear-based habits with acts of generosity and support.

We encourage others to see their failures not as stumbling blocks but as building blocks that can be used to help others. A correct perspective inspires them to ask, *"What tools (building blocks) have I been given to function with?"*

Inspired by how many tools they have to help others; they change their focus from being self-conscious to being conscious of other's needs. As their focus changes, seeing their tools within themselves opens their eyes to their value and worth and how they can use them to help others. The more they see others positively affected using their tools, the more they desire to help them. Their joy at seeing others benefit breaks their cycle of being so self-conscious. Overcoming self-consciousness inspires those facing challenges to share their valuable life lessons.

Being inspired to humble themselves and share their valuable life lessons with others prevents them from falling into the trap of self-consciousness. They are free from self-consciousness and bring hope to others who feel hopeless and trapped. Seeing the hope they can bring through sharing their life lessons inspires them to keep helping others struggling with failures. By sharing their own experiences, they encourage others to confront their past mistakes and grow from them. Seeing their mistakes positively rather than negatively shows others how to be released from their torment. Instead of being tormented by their mistakes, they are inspired to ask: *"What can I learn through my mistakes to help others?"*

They inspire others to be mindful of the words they say about themselves or others, especially when they make mistakes. Realizing how powerful words can be to themselves or others. Words can powerfully build up or tear down ourselves or others. They inspire others to respond positively to words by teaching them how words can affect people. Learning to respond positively to words prevents them from negatively overreacting to words. By learning to respond positively to words, they help others become more confident to share their life lessons and use the tools they have.

THE CHALLENGE OF BEING
OVERLY SELF-CONSCIOUS

They act boldly by being willing to share their life lessons instead of being so self-conscious of how others may negatively respond to them. Their boldness to share their painful life lessons allows them to stop talking negatively about themselves by seeing how valuable they are to others. Their positive outlook and courage bring them out of their self-conscious isolation, fed by fear and torment. Viewing their mistakes positively inspires them to get the help they need to avoid repeating their mistakes in the future. Through the support of the right people, they are equipped to function more effectively to help others.

Their ability to work better gives them the confidence to keep pressing forward rather than retreating in defeat. By avoiding negative criticism, they excel and become more secure in their abilities. Their effectiveness and security make them productive and creative as they help others. We inspire positive reactions to challenges. Rather than letting their words have negative control over others, they choose to respond positively with their words. Encouraging others through their words inspires them to see their unique vision and purpose. Seeing their uniqueness and purpose, they use their words to respond positively, not negatively. Using their words positively enables them to direct, inspire, or motivate others.

This correct use of their words breaks the negative pattern of using them to dominate, intimidate, or manipulate others. Using their words correctly allows them to talk or instruct without being controlling or overpowering. Knowing how powerful words can affect them inspires us to pay careful attention to their negative self-talk and stop it before it destroys them or others. They quit negative self-talk by silencing doubts, disqualification, and self-consciousness. They silence the negative words by no longer comparing themselves to others.

As they refrain from comparing themselves with others, they are prevented from falling into jealousy and envy. Instead of succumbing to jealousy towards those around us, they seek assistance from them in their areas of need. Their willingness to help others, rather than harboring jealousy or envy, allows them to benefit from others' strengths. Benefiting from their strengths gives them greater confidence in their own identity. By embracing support from others instead of feeling jealous or envious, they become uniquely equipped to function most effectively and take calculated risks. Reaching out to others, rather than succumbing to jealousy, makes them transparent and vulnerable, fostering connections rather than isolation.

CONCLUSION

Being overly self-conscious can quickly stop people from fulfilling what they have been destined to do. For the first eighteen years of my life, I disqualified myself from doing many things I should have been doing. However, things changed after I had a radical mindset change and saw how I needed to give people what I should be. It has been a joy to push past my self-consciousness and share what I can with others, even if I can't do it perfectly. I have found that people are more concerned about your heart than you not being able to do something perfectly. Letting go of being self-conscious has freed me up to be myself and give others what I can. I no longer find myself living in regret and shame. I have learned to be more mindful of my words towards myself and not to respond negatively to my mistakes.

APPLICATION

1. How has self-consciousness held you back?

2. What can you do to stop it?

3. Who do you feel most self-conscious about being around?

4. What does your self-talk reflect when you make mistakes?

5. Who can you be a cheerleader to, helping them overcome their self-consciousness?

CHAPTER SIXTEEN
CHALLENGE OF BITTERNESS

"Hi, spaz. What's wrong with you spastic? Why do you walk so funny? Why are you talking like that? What's wrong with you?"

My bitterness towards my peers and God grew as I continually heard this. They ridiculed me daily in this way, not understanding my difficulties with slow muscular movement. Their continual ridicule made me think, why are they making fun of my challenges with my slow muscular movement? Why have I been made this way? Not having the answers, I needed to answer these questions as the years passed caused bitterness to consume me like poison, making me resentful. I was bitter and resentful towards those ridiculing me and towards God for making me the way I perceived myself to be.

BREAKDOWN

CYCLE OF BITTERNESS AND ANGER

We feel bitter towards those who reject us, ourselves, and eventually towards God, leading to self-hatred and resentment. Our bitterness allows anger issues to start growing. Causing us to feel like victims isolated in self-pity. Becoming passive-aggressive or silent rather than communicating.

BITTERNESS RESTRICTS US

We start becoming bitter about who we are and the weaknesses we see within ourselves. This wrong focus restricts and hinders us from functioning correctly. By restricting ourselves, we become uncomfortable being who we should be and are blinded to our unique qualities.

BITTERNESS LEADS TO RESENTMENT

Our bitterness and resentment make us struggle with our circumstances, hindering us from being able to accept and love ourselves. The longer we allow our bitterness and resentment to grow within us, the more deeply rooted it becomes.

We become bitter towards those who reject us or even towards God. We become bitter and resentful towards Him for allowing us to feel the way we do about ourselves. We struggle to recognize and deal with our bitterness and resentfulness without the help of others. If we don't get the help needed soon enough, it leads to frustration and anger.

Our frustration and anger often rise so quickly toward ourselves that it surprises us. Not realizing why, we become so frustrated and angry with ourselves and others, allowing our negative feelings to fester. Surprised by our growing anger, we ask ourselves why and seek help to overcome it. We know seeking help is essential to overcome our bitterness and resentment, causing our ongoing growing negativity. Our negative actions, reactions, and words hurt us and those we are in contact with daily. Sadly, as we will see in our next challenge, hurting people hurts people in the same way that rejected people reject people. I found this true as I began rejecting the ones who rejected me.

When I came in contact with them, I would put up an invisible wall of separation between us in self-confidence as a defense. I thought, "I will no longer let them hurt me through their rejection." Knowing I still had to be in contact with them daily, I rejected them by choosing not to interact positively with them. Those with challenges may make bad choices and feel increasingly bitter and resentful for doing so. Eventually, we may doubt our ability to overcome these feelings. Our feeling of hopelessness then allows a victim mentality to develop. Our victim mentality or mindset then causes the vicious cycle within ourselves to grow even more.

Eventually, seeing our challenges with bitterness too massive to overcome, we wallow in pity. Having a "woe is me," "don't you feel sorrow for poor me" victim attitude. Being negative can cause anger towards ourselves and others, affecting our relationships. Our relationships with others become strained, as we are not open and honest about how they make us feel. Our lack of openness and honesty feeds into the challenge of defiance as we remain silent instead of expressing our true feelings.

We looked at the challenge of defiance in the previous section of our journey together. Our defiance and lack of honesty hinder us from positively reaching out to others in positive ways. Hence, we either ignore or openly reject reaching out and building healthy relationships. We use past hurt and rejection to not interact with certain people, and we use passive aggression to protect ourselves from further hurt or rejection by others. However, sadly, it simply leads us into further isolation, hurt, pain, and issues we addressed in the first chapter of our journey together, where we saw how we tried to build walls to protect ourselves from the pain of our challenges.

Feeling like a victim makes us go back behind the invisible walls we talked about in our first challenge. Our challenge of walls causes us to feel isolated, lonely, and like we are in a prison again. Feeling bad about ourselves and others can cause us to make bad choices, leading to bitterness and resentment. By feeding on our victim mentality and negative emotions within our souls, we make these challenges seem much more significant than they are or should be. We struggle with bitterness and resentment, wondering if we can ever overcome them and be free of our anger.

The deeper it gets rooted within us, the harder it becomes for us to function; therefore, we think we lack value or purpose. Our self-rejection deepens as we believe the lies about who we are. We buy into the lies we hear through others' rejection or our rejection of ourselves. We battle to see ourselves as we should. Our blindness to our abilities stops us from trying to do what we can and keeps us stuck in the lies of what we think we can't do. I directly link this to the self-pity challenge we studied earlier.

We feel bitter and sorry for ourselves, struggle to get along with others, and deal with our circumstances. Because of our inner struggles, we focus on the negative aspects of our lives instead of embracing our situation and making the most of it. Negativity and bitterness make us develop a false belief system about ourselves. Wrong beliefs about who we are make us feel flawed, leading to a deep-seated disdain toward ourselves and those around us.

In this last section of our journey, we will address negative attitudes and responses caused by our wrong self-beliefs. We studied the challenge of disdain in an earlier chapter of our journey together. We saw how much of a challenge it can become. When we don't address the challenges of disdain, it can lead to bitterness. I suggest you revisit the chapter on disdain after this one, as bitterness is closely linked to disdain. The longer we allow our bitterness and disdain to continue, the more likely it will lead to resentment challenges.

BREAKTHROUGH

AVOIDING IT

Recognize our uniqueness and choose to change our negative attitudes. We let go of our angry victim mentality, resist isolating ourselves in self-pity, and choose to forgive. We develop relationships without being driven by aggressive disdain.

SHOWING UNDERSTANDING COMPASSION

Understanding and compassion toward ourselves and others are keys to overcoming bitterness and resentment. Understanding and having compassion help us deal with our wrong-formed attitudes toward ourselves, others, and God. Understanding and compassion change our negative attitudes.

ACCEPTING OURSELVES AND FORGIVING

We begin accepting our uniqueness and responding positively instead of reacting negatively. Being at peace within enables us to show love and compassion to others and avoid negativity. We forgive ourselves, others, and God, becoming peaceful, loving, and compassionate.

We can achieve peace by accepting our uniqueness and learning to respond instead of reacting. We can take our differences peacefully instead of becoming bitter and resentful. Being at peace within ourselves causes us to respond to others in loving, compassionate ways instead of having bitter resentment towards them. Choosing to react positively to rejection helps us respond in caring and positive ways instead of negative ways.

We become more positive towards ourselves and others, radically changing our attitude. Instead of rejecting and reacting bitterly, we accept ourselves and respond positively. A positive response to ourselves, others, and our circumstances reduce our bitter, angry aggression. Our positive response helps us release bitterness and positively impacts ourselves and others.

Releasing my self-rejection, self-hatred, and bitterness by embracing my unique qualities led to one of my most significant breakthroughs. It was so profound that I can still remember the night I had my breakthrough as though it were yesterday. That night, I embraced myself with cerebral palsy limitations and changed my attitude toward others' reactions. I ignored a student who told me to write faster during biology class. When he came and apologized a week later, I said: "Thank you. I accept myself the way I am, and I am working on my past negative attitudes, which need to change." It became a significant moment of triumph for me over my self-hatred and bitterness toward those who had rejected me for being different.

Letting go of negative attitudes towards ourselves and others can empower us to make the necessary changes. Our change comes from being willing to ask ourselves the hard questions needed to break through our negative cycles. Reflecting on our answers can help us see things differently and overcome bitterness and resentment. Seeing things differently and desiring to make the changes we have to, even the hard ones, moves us forward positively. Wishing to keep moving forward should lead to us working on an excellent strategic action plan of positive action. We use positive steps to eliminate negative attitudes developed from bitterness and resentment.

We start with the most challenging tasks, confident that success with those will lead to winning with the others. Looking at our bitterness and challenges correctly helps us stay calm by seeing them as unconquerable. Reflecting on how bitterness and resentment affect relationships can help those facing challenges. We realize that bitterness and resentment have adverse effects. So, we focus on making practical positive changes. We begin practically with our wrong attitudes towards how we see and react to ourselves. We embrace our uniqueness as we reverse our false perceptions of how we have viewed ourselves.

We let go of our bitterness or resentment towards ourselves by embracing our identity and specifically dealing with our bitterness and resentment to avoid adverse effects. As we see how destructive bitterness and resentment are, it shocks us into taking the actions needed to stop its negative impact on us and others. Seeing how it leads to unforgiveness causes us to work on forgiving ourselves, others, and even God if we need to do that. We become less angry and more peaceful by forgiving ourselves, others, and God.

By reflecting on our actions in a relaxed state, we become less bitter, resentful, and angry. Positive self-evaluation helps us respond positively to rejection instead of reacting aggressively—our new perspective of valuing ourselves more changes how we interact with others. Our proper view of ourselves helps us see how life's challenges can make us tender instead of tough, better instead of bitter. Instead of seeing life's difficulties as sour lemons, we see how many we have to make lemonade with. Our newfound positivity allows us to enjoy life to the full as an overcomer, not as a bitter, resentful, angry victim.

Through seeing things positively, we reach out to others instead of isolating ourselves from them. Positive interactions with them help us let go of negative emotions and find joy. The more we enjoy positive interactions with others, the less we desire to return to our bitter, resentful, angry ways. We repair old relationships and create new ones free of bitterness, resentment, and anger. As our new relationships grow, we learn to speak up when needed and fight the urge to go into passive aggression or willful destruction of defiance.

INSPIRE

CULTIVATE POSITIVE ATTITUDES

We inspire them to have positive attitudes towards themselves and others. We show them how a changed attitude free of bitterness and resentment brings a life free of isolation and pity. We inspire them to see how powerful good relationships can be in helping them become better people, free of anger and filled with peace.

BE KIND AND COMPASSIONATE

Being inspired to show kindness and compassion allows them to overcome bitterness and resentment. Inspiring them to let go of any negativity and judgmental attitudes and see things correctly instead of through the lenses of bitterness and unforgiveness.

SEE THINGS DIFFERENTLY

It inspires them to see themselves, others, and even God differently and to look at things positively instead of being judgmental and negative. Their new way of seeing things inspires them to overcome their victim mentality and see things as they should.

We inspire others to be kind and compassionate towards themselves and others. Seeing how their understanding and compassion can change their negative attitudes towards themselves. Understanding and compassion can prevent them from judging others who act negatively or react negatively toward them. Inspired by our compassion, they reflect on how they treat people with handicaps or those who are different. Inspiring them to think about how those with a handicap can only change their wrong thinking about themselves, not how they were created. It inspires them to see how changing their thinking can transform their hearts and attitudes towards themselves and others.

Our changed thinking patterns inspire them to stop negatively reacting in bitter, resentful, angry ways. Instead of negatively reacting, we inspire them to respond positively, learning not to be as hard on themselves or others for being different. They can come to peace with their uniqueness by responding instead of reacting. Being at peace with ourselves inspires others to accept their differences instead of being bitter, resentful, or angry about them. We inspire them to respond in loving, compassionate ways instead of bitter resentment and anger.

We inspire them to love and show compassion instead of bitterness toward themselves and others. We inspire them and others around them to have a radical attitude change. Changing their attitude brings about self-acceptance and positivity instead of bitterness, resentment, and anger. Through our lack of aggression and anger, we inspire them and others. Instead of being bitter, resentful, and angry, they are inspired to remain optimistic and inspire others. Our positive attitude inspires others to let go of bitterness, resentment, and anger.

Our ability to let go of our negative attitudes inspires others watching us, inspiring them to do the same. Empowering them to change their attitudes despite their physical limitations and inspiring them to ask themselves the hard questions. These questions are needed to break their negative cycles of bitterness, resentment, and anger. Their answers inspire them to work on their issues instead of running from them. Inspiring them to see themselves as overcoming, not trapped victims. They become inspired to change and break free, making the changes, even the hardest ones, to move forward positively. Inspired by their positive progress and victories, they seek the right strategic action plan of positive action to help them in the future. We inspire them to release their negative attitudes and mindsets through personal victories.

We inspire them to work on their most overwhelming challenges, first knowing if they can conquer these, then conquering the rest will be easier. We inspire them to have a positive outlook and take action instead of being stuck in their bitterness, resentment, anger, and hopelessness. Being inspired that they can conquer their bitterness, resentment, anger, and negativity helps them see how this has negatively affected them and others around them. Their insight inspires them to take positive actions to reverse things. They aim to make positive changes for themselves and others to combat bitterness, resentment, and anger.

Being practical and strategic changes their negative attitudes towards themselves and others. They celebrate their individuality by changing their view of themselves, embracing their uniqueness, and no longer seeing what is happening through their victim mentality. By embracing their unique identity, they let go of their bitterness, resentment, and anger toward themselves and allow others to celebrate them. Seeing our positive changes inspires them to let go of their bitterness, resentment, and anger by practically dealing with it and its effect on everyone.

We inspire others to follow our lead by dealing with our bitterness and preventing them from festering. Seeing how negatively their bitterness impacts them and others shocks them. The shock inspires them to take action, find specific solutions, and look for any unforgiveness caused by allowing bitterness and resentment to grow within them. They are inspired to forgive themselves, others, or God practically. Their practical actions lead to peace and freedom from bitterness, resentment, and anger. Their peace and joy inspire them to rethink how they react to people who cause them to be bitter, resentful, and angry.

Their positive results inspire them to respond positively to rejection instead of reacting aggressively. Their freedom and inspiration cause them to see things differently, thinking positively about themselves and others. Looking at things positively inspires them to face challenges without negativity. Their fresh sight and inspiration to see how unique they are helps them become tender instead of tough and better instead of bitter, resentful, and angry. They see their tough challenges as sour lemons or opportunities to make lemonade.

Thanks to their new inspired perspective, they can see things through new lenses. Their new perspective enables them to enjoy life as an overcomer, not a bitter victim. Inspiring them to reach out to others instead of isolating themselves. They defeat their negativity by seeking joy in positive interactions with others and God. The joy of their new friendships inspires them to enjoy even more positive interactions with others instead of being bitter towards them. The peace, joy, and freedom they find now fill their lives, so they become determined never to allow bitterness, resentment, or anger to return. Their inspiration leads them to repair relationships broken by their bitterness. Being on guard not to let bitterness contaminate their new healthy relationships. Positive relationships inspire them to fight the urge to be passive-aggressive.

CONCLUSION

Oh, what a joy to finally discover who I was and that I was not a spastic retard or made to be everybody's clown to mock and tease. I found my uniqueness and was finally happy to be who I was. Accepting who I was opened my eyes to see my uniqueness and that I did not need to compete with others. Instead, I was to compliment them and help them. I began working hard to change the wrong attitudes I had about myself. I came to peace with changing what I could and being at peace with what I could not. My attitude changes radically altered my relationships with those around me, and I began working positively with them instead of feeling like the victim when I was around them.

APPLICATION

1. How confident are you in who you are?

2. What abilities do you have that are unique to you?

3. Do you find yourself competing or complementing those around you?

4. What things about you make you feel like a victim?

5. What attitudes about yourself are you going to start changing after this chapter?

CHAPTER SEVENTEEN
THE CHALLENGE OF
REJECTING PEOPLE

"Ignore him. He is just a spastic retard."

Hearing this continually said by one of my closest family members who would say this to my siblings caused me such hurt that I responded by rejecting us. I tried as hard as I could to cut them out of my life emotionally as I put up my emotional walls of self-protection to try not to be hurt by them. Once again, I wanted to protect myself by rejecting them for rejecting me. Although I interacted with them daily, I cut them off through silent defiance and my negative attitude toward them. Even though their rejection was incorrect, my adverse reaction to them was just as wrong. Causing a challenge for me not to reject those who rejected me.

BREAKDOWN

WE FIND OURSELVES REJECTING OTHERS

Our rejection of others and ourselves causes us to keep others at arm's length. Our rejection leads to us becoming judgmental or critical of them. As judgmental criticism grows, we become intolerant, lack compassion, and overreact.

BECOMING FEAR-DRIVEN

Fear can lead us to build walls around ourselves, be fearful of people, become co-dependent on others, lack clear

216

boundaries, and become performance-driven. Leading to a deep-seated rejection of others and ourselves.

MISUNDERSTANDING CORRECTIONS

We choose to respond to rejection by tolerating the rejecter instead of understanding and working with them. Our tolerance of them makes us lack compassionate care or concern for them. This directly impacts our relationship with them.

When we face intense rejection challenges, we reject others and ourselves. We find ourselves rejecting others for rejecting us and rejecting ourselves in the process. We reject ourselves because of the deep hurt caused by our rejection of ourselves or by being constantly rejected by others. Our self-rejection then leads to us rejecting others who view us as different, disabled, or for having a handicap. Just as hurting people hurts people, rejected people reject people. Causing a vicious negative cycle to develop. Our struggle with self-rejection is also directly linked to our disdain for ourselves. We addressed this challenge earlier, and this negative attitude wants to poison all the other attitudes we discuss in this section on bad attitudes. Our adverse reaction to being rejected by others makes it hard for us to be open to receiving what we should from them.

Our wrong attitudes of rejection towards ourselves and others hinder us from working effectively with them, as we choose to have as little as possible to do with them because of our fear of rejection. We cannot effectively work with them as our rejection of them directly affects our ability to communicate with them as we should. As we choose to reject those who reject us, we keep them at arm's length emotionally, not connecting with them as we should. We may be around them, but we choose not to communicate with them as we should, fearing they may hurt or reject us if we interact with them.

In our first section, we saw five adverse reactions that stem from fear when we face rejection challenges. Fear can lead us to build walls around ourselves, be fearful of people, become co-dependent on others, lack clear boundaries, and become performance-driven. These five adverse reactions eventually lead to this deep-seated rejection of others and ourselves.

This rejection of others and ourselves causes us to become judgmental and critical of others and ourselves. We judge people quickly without getting to know them and their true motives. Our judgmental criticism hinders our ability to develop friendships and get to know them as we should. Being judgmental and critical of others and ourselves affects our ability to work with others in healthy ways as we should. Rather than positively engaging with others, we distance ourselves from them. Our negative attitude towards them causes us to keep others at arm's length, creating a hostile environment.

The adverse climate directly affects our productivity and the productivity of others. It is hard for us to ask for or receive help from authority figures because we are so afraid of being rejected by them. We reject anyone who tries to correct us and refuse to submit to them as we should. We have so negatively programmed ourselves to see all correction as a personal rejection that we react negatively.

Earlier, we addressed the challenge of not accepting correction.

When others sense and feel our uncaring tolerance of them, it sadly causes more rejection. As rejected people, we overreact to others, rejecting them when they remind us of painful experiences we've had in the past or present. We react negatively because of their past or present painful memories. These painful memories often cause us to react too quickly without thinking about how wrongly we are acting in a hostile, unloving way to others' rejection.

BREAKTHROUGH

WE FIND OURSELVES RESPONDING INSTEAD OF REACTING

We choose to no longer reject others or ourselves. We draw close to others by embracing them with compassion. Replacing our judgmental criticism of them with a caring attitude, desiring to reach out to them.

BUILDING EMOTIONAL CONNECTIONS

We consciously reach out, especially when we fear being rejected, to connect with others emotionally, preventing us from keeping them at arm's length. We connect in a positive, effective way, allowing them to do the same.

ACCEPTING OF OTHERS

By taking time to get to know each other as we should, we are prevented from being critical or judgmental as we get to know each other, enabling us to accept one another and form deeper friendships free from the fear of rejection.

We recognize our battle of getting into a destructive cycle of rejecting others when we feel rejected by them and break the cycle before it's too late. Having seen the negativity that comes from our self-rejection, we accept ourselves and have an attitude of self-acceptance by valuing ourselves. Our correct view of ourselves changes our views and actions toward those we encounter daily. Viewing ourselves as we should enables us to accept people who may not be able to see past our being different, disabled, or handicapped. Knowing how easy it is for hurting people to hurt people or for rejected people to reject people.

Therefore, we begin working on our hurts or rejection so it does not hinder our future relationships. Taking the time needed to evaluate how we view our differences, disabilities, or handicaps. Knowing that our thinking will directly affect our behavior, actions, and responses to those we encounter daily. Stinking thinking is often easier recognized by those around us listening to our words, than ourselves, and we sometimes need a wake-up call to get us back on track.

Connecting with others breaks down our walls of fear of being hurt or rejected, allowing us to build solid relationships that can last for years. As we saw in our first chapter, fear can negatively impact our relationships with others in several ways. The more significant the breakthrough we have through our newfound positive relationships, the easier it becomes for us to overcome building walls, living in fear, being co-dependent on others, having no boundaries, and being performance-driven.

Our ongoing friendship allows us to work well together instead of being critical and judgmental. As we work together, we break out of our false comfort zone of isolation and get closer to each other. Working together in harmony as good friends creates a positive environment for us to work in, which replaces the negative environment created by rejecting one another.

This new positive environment directly affects our productivity and the productivity of those we are working with. Instead of rejecting others' help, we submit to their authority, knowing they have our best interests at heart. Our willingness to submit to them and their willingness to submit to us makes it easy to ask for help when needed and to receive correction from each other. We can submit and be corrected without seeing all corrections as personal rejections. Our rejection of correction was a challenge we addressed earlier, and it is connected to the negative attitudes we've seen in past challenges.

We must change our attitude towards those we perceive as rejecting us. Choosing to reach out to them in caring ways instead of tolerating them. Winning them over with our caring compassion and genuine concern for their needs. Our compassion and concern cause acceptance and draw them closer so we can develop an ongoing friendship with them. Instead of dwelling on our painful past experiences from rejection, which makes us unapproachable, we dwell on the joy coming from our new positive friendships. Our joy-filled relationships give us hope to move forward positively instead of staying stuck in our negative ones. Our positivity allows us not to reject others but to stop and think about why they may be reacting the way they are. Being mindful of others' hurts leads us to respond in loving ways filled with genuine care instead of reacting to them in unloving, harmful ways.

By taking the time needed to consider our actions or reactions as well as the actions or reactions of others, we master this rejection challenge, helping others to do the same. Overcoming our self-rejection enables us to receive from others as we should. Identifying our harmful reactions and actions towards ourselves and others makes us more sensitive to our self-rejection. We become open to receiving from others through mastering our self-rejection and learning to accept ourselves. Our self-acceptance and openness to receive from others cause us to connect with them correctly from the heart instead of rejecting them.

As we connect with others, instead of rejecting them, we allow them to get to know us, and we get to know them before rejecting them in critical, judgmental ways. By building relationships instead of being critical and judgmental, we get to know each other's hearts. Our heart connection allows us to be open to receiving correct from each other without overreacting negatively. We both benefit by helping each other see what needs to be corrected. Leading us to place importance on correction and people in authority instead of rejecting it. Placing the proper importance on correction causes us to celebrate those willing to help us see what we were too blind to see on our own. We allow others to help us and show kindness to others struggling with similar issues. Instead of being critical and judgmental of them, we show compassion and understanding, knowing how hard it was to deal with our past rejections and hurts.

Through exercising self-control, we no longer use emotional blackmail to control those we fear may reject us. Our self-control and lack of fear allow us to respond correctly and lovingly rather than in negatively controlling ways. Exercising self-control helps us deal with rejection more effectively. Our openness to being corrected leads us to seek help when needed, leading to better judgment.

INSPIRE

CELEBRATING OTHERS

By showing them how to draw close to celebrate others instead of keeping them at arm's length. Replacing their critical, judgmental attitude toward them with genuine, caring compassion.

FOSTERING HELP AND GROWTH

They are inspired to embrace their identity and connect with others on a deep, heart level. These deep relationships inspire them to become less judgmental and not to reject others too quickly, especially when they are corrected.

LETTING GO OF FEAR

Help received from others enables them to overcome their fears. Their freedom releases them from using emotional blackmail to control. They patiently wait to avoid adverse reactions to their fears.

By embracing their identity, they can genuinely connect with others on a deep heart level. Inspired by their deep and ongoing relationships, they become less judgmental of one another as they get to know each other's hearts. They are inspired not to be critical of or reject others before getting to know them and what motivates them. Being inspired not to be judgmental and critical and seeing how much others can help them inspires them to want to let others correct and help them when needed. The more they allow themselves to be corrected and helped, the more they value it. Desiring to receive correction and support from others, especially those in authority.

We inspire others not to reject themselves or others when feeling rejected but to accept themselves as unique and special. We are willing to embrace our uniqueness and change our wrong attitudes about ourselves. Their attitude change will inspire others to make the same radical attitude adjustments.

The more their attitude about themselves changes about who they are, the less they will reject others or be critical or judgmental of them. Their self-acceptance inspires others to celebrate their uniqueness without being rejected by them. As others celebrate them, they begin celebrating others instead of rejecting them, as they had done in the past. The longer they celebrate others, the more it inspires them to accept their uniqueness and see how special they are. Being celebrated correctly inspires them to be more accepting of themselves and others.

This positive cycle then breaks the negative cycle of hurting themselves and others. As they allow this positive cycle to continue, they become more open to receiving unique abilities and talents from others. Their willingness to receive from others and seeing how much stronger it makes them inspired them to accept others around them and ask for their help. Emotional connection with others inspires solid relationships and friendships. They become more inspired to accept themselves and others through building these positive relationships.

Their inspiration causes them to become compassionate instead of tolerant of others. Their compassion leads to positive interaction with others, resulting in collaboration instead of rejection of one another. Working together positively with others inspires them to be kind and avoid rejection, leading to positive results and a great work environment.

They are inspired to control their emotions by working together positively instead of using their emotions negatively to reject and control each other. They are inspired to get to know their friends and see how they can help them before being critical and judgmental of them. Knowing someone's heart before rejecting them can prevent adverse reactions, especially if they have been hurt or are hurting.

They are inspired to get to know others and become more effective at what they do with their help. The positive help from others enables them to overcome many of the fears we addressed in our first chapter. Their freedom from their fears releases them from using emotional blackmail to control those they fear may reject them. By not using emotional blackmail, they are inspired to respond correctly in love instead of reacting negatively, driven by their fears. Waiting, thinking, and listening to trusted people's advice helps avoid adverse reactions and fear.

By responding positively instead of negatively, they are inspired to no longer ruin relationships but respond with care, improving their present and future relationships.

CONCLUSION

Positive relationships with others require getting past rejection and being distanced. Good relationships increase our ability to work with others through emotional connection. Changing our attitude helps us work together effectively and achieve our goals. I changed my attitude towards them when I realized I had built a wall between myself and a family member who rejected me. I changed my perspective and took a practical step to correct my wrongful actions towards them. I wrote a letter to apologize for rejecting them and distancing myself emotionally from them. Even though they didn't respond to my apology, it still positively affected me and stopped me from distancing myself from them.

APPLICATION

1. Is there anyone or others you have rejected because of past rejection or hurt from them?

2. How do you plan to make things right with them?

3. Is there someone who reminds you of a past hurt stopping you from forming new relationships?

4. How open are you to receiving correction or help from others?

5. How important is it to have a positive working environment with others?

CHAPTER EIGHTEEN
THE CHALLENGE OF
BEING HYPERSENSITIVE

"Oh no, we laughing at me again for my slow movements and speech."

That was going through my mind as I entered a room full of young people I had not met before. They started laughing when I entered. My immediate reaction was to assume we were laughing at me, as that had been my experience with young people over the years. I had that adverse reaction, as I had programmed myself to be hypersensitive to young people's responses to my cerebral palsy. My hypersensitivity caused me to overreact negatively before making sure they were reacting to me.

BREAKDOWN

OVERREACT TO TRIGGERS

We overreact immediately to trigger situations, reacting too quickly from our emotions. We react strongly to perceived rejection or possible rejection. We lack humility, becoming insensitive to people's needs and avoiding specific individuals to whom we react in fear.

LACK DISCERNMENT

Fearful of being around certain people, they lack discernment and only want to be in smaller groups. We react in fear when reminded of past rejection and being uncomfortable and comfortable around certain people.

STRUGGLE WITH HONESTY

Our overreaction due to fear causes us to struggle to be honest with others. Instead of being open and honest, humbling ourselves, and letting others get to know us, we hide from them in fear.

Our hypersensitivity makes us critical and judgmental around certain groups or individuals. By allowing ourselves to become judgmental, we immediately put a barrier between ourselves and others we fear. Our fear and barriers hinder our ability to interact with those we should reach out to and build relationships with. Therefore, we do not work effectively with the ones we should work with or receive valuable help from them because of our barriers and hypersensitivity. We react when others tease, belittle, or mock us, so others must be extra careful around us. Past negative experiences can cause us to be hypersensitive and overreact to specific situations. We overreact without assessing the problem because of our negative past experiences, hurt, or rejection.

Our hypersensitivity causes us to neglect the needs of others because we are too focused on our feelings or sensitivities. Focusing too much on ourselves makes others feel neglected and unimportant. Our inward self-focus and wrong attitude toward those around us we should be helping and working with cause us not to celebrate and recognize them. Instead of celebrating them, we create a barrier and selfishly withdraw from them, thinking that they cannot reject or hurt us if we ignore and withdraw from them.

Struggling struggle to express ourselves makes us afraid of opening up to some people we fear. Our fear causes us not to get too close to them, thinking that they may reject us if they get to see our weaknesses. The longer we remain at an arm's length away from those we should interact and work with, the harder we find it to work with them as a team. We fear working with others because we are so hypersensitive, that we overreact too quickly, which can be embarrassing. Our hypersensitivity can cause us to lack righteous judgment, refusing the help and wisdom others have to give us. Our lack of judgment and discernment results in us needing to know which group or groups we may fit into or be a part desire to be a part of. We fear getting involved because we need to know where we fit in or should be, especially with large groups we need to be acquainted with.

BREAKTHROUGH

UNDERSTAND OUR TRIGGERS AND REACTIONS

We learn to wait and correctly assess the situation before responding or reacting strongly. We become sensitive to the needs of others and choose not to avoid specific individuals by reacting fearfully.

GROW IN OUR DISCERNMENT

By becoming sensitive to others' needs, we discern situations correctly and learn to be comfortable in all groups. We also become aware of who we overreact to and why.

REACH OUT TO OTHERS

We learn to calm down before reacting negatively, shifting our focus to recognize any fear of rejection, working on our fears instead of running from our fears, and resulting in a welcoming, united environment for everyone.

Our breakthrough helps us identify our trigger points or groups and know who we need to learn to become comfortable with. We study what people or groups we most strongly react to and why we have become overly sensitive to those people. We find this out by checking who we find ourselves most sensitive and careful around. Then, we are willing to ask ourselves the hard questions about why we feel uncomfortable around them.

We respond differently based on our past hurts or rejection from others. It was young people I was most sensitive being around, so I had to learn not to react too quickly to them as they would laugh at me. My hypersensitivity made me always think they were laughing at me, even when they were not. I had to learn to be willing to open up to them before becoming critical or judgmental of them and making a conscious decision not to put up my barriers and walls to protect myself.

We break through our hypersensitivity challenge by reviewing the answers to our questions and choosing not to put up our barriers when we come in contact with our trigger group. Instead of allowing our barriers to stop us from interacting with them, we choose to reach out to them and start building relationships with them. Our willful action is a massive step for us, and it is critical not to let our fears paralyze us. By reaching out to develop and build these relationships, we find ourselves becoming much more effective at what we must do. By getting to know them through our relationship with them, we can see how they can help us be most productive and overcome our hypersensitive fears. Therefore, we start working effectively with the ones we should work with, receiving valuable help from them.

We learn to respond instead of react when we feel rejected by our trigger groups or groups. By working through our past negative experiences, we remain calm instead of overreacting to specific situations that get us riled up. Remaining calm enables us to assess situations positively rather than react negatively because of past experiences, hurt, or rejection.

We turn our hypersensitivity from ourselves and begin using them to help meet the needs of others, becoming more aware of their needs than our feelings or sensitivities. By focusing on their needs and feelings, we allow them to feel important and cared for by us. Our outward focus motivates us to help others in need and celebrate them. We break through any barriers by celebrating them and making them feel special, drawing us closer to them.

By paying them positive attention, we overcame our fears that wanted to distract us from them, calming our rejection and hurt. Rather than trying to ignore people, we choose to talk things through with them or face any unresolved rejection hurts that have to be addressed. Being open and honest with them and ourselves transforms our future relationships. Our openness and honesty let others know how we feel and what makes us want to hide from them in fear. By humbling ourselves in this way, we find peace within ourselves and with those we want to hide from.

Our openness and honesty help us overcome our struggles to express ourselves and make us less afraid of opening up to the people we fear may hurt or reject us. Instead of allowing fear to hinder us from reaching out and getting too close to them, we allow them to see our weaknesses, trusting they will not reject us. By drawing close to them, we can positively interact and work with them freely.

Recognizing and valuing how they can help us as part of the team. We overcome our fear of working with others by not being hypersensitive and impatient with them or ourselves. Instead of being embarrassed by our weaknesses or flaws, we allow them to be exposed so others can help us with them. Our openness, honesty, and humility, together with their help, cause us to grow in wisdom and sound judgment. Our sound wisdom and judgment make us more discerning of how vital it is to work with as many as possible.

Each group has unique wisdom to impart, helping us become the most effective individuals or as a team. Rather than being overly picky about what group or groups we are willing to work with, we desire to be a part of any that can help us. Through our openness to working with others and learning from them, we find ourselves fitting in with many more people and getting acquainted with them, whether the groups are big or small.

Through our willingness to find where we fit best, we not only find ourselves getting helped, but we can also help

233

others in the team. By getting acquainted with others around us and helping them positively, we learn to become more sensitive to their needs instead of staying stuck on our own. The joy of seeing how willing they are to respond when we reach out to help them causes our fears to dissipate, being replaced by genuine compassion.

No longer driven by our fears, we can redirect our sensibilities in the right way to be helpful to others. Becoming so focused on their needs, we forget about our weaknesses and self-disqualification of ourselves. When we build up others, we become more attentive to their needs, resulting in greater acceptance by them despite our failures. We accept others instead of being hypersensitive to them, which stops our tendency to be critical or judgmental of ourselves or others. As we stop being critical and judgmental of ourselves and others, we find ourselves compassionate towards ourselves.

By becoming compassionate, we find our fears of rejection replaced by a desire to engage with others and help them as much as possible. Their positive response to our genuine care helps us overcome our fear of interacting with others, especially those we do not know well.

By mastering our hypersensitivity rather than staying self-focused on our needs, we start helping others without being asked to, as we are so sensitive to their needs. Their positive responses to our sensitivity to their needs inspire us to continue helping them and bring us great joy and a sense of fulfillment. We find our fear of being rejected by others being replaced by such fulfillment that we no longer want to isolate ourselves but rather start looking for who we can help next.

Helping others breaks our harmful tendencies to isolate ourselves and opens us up to being more people-conscious than self-conscious. As we reach out to help others, we open up to ourselves, being open and honest about our strengths and weaknesses instead of hiding our weaknesses from others.

Being open and honest draws people towards us rather than pushing them away. Our openness and transparency unite us with them, causing us to work with them rather than run from them as we are aware of their needs. Seeing our caring hearts and willingness to help them despite our inabilities causes them to identify with us and to respond positively. Working in unity as we identify with each other causes us to grow in our discernment instead of withdrawing from each other in fear. This discernment leads to more excellent positive responses to each other's needs, making it a joy to be together and learn how to help others overcome their hypersensitivity.

INSPIRE

LEARNING TO WAIT

Wait and correctly assess the situation before responding or strongly overreacting to certain triggers. Become aware and sensitive to the needs of others. Reaching out with loving care instead of reacting in fear.

GROW IN DISCERNMENT

We inspire others to reach out positively to those around them, grow in their discernment, and respond with care to others' needs without fear. Not reacting negatively and withdrawing, but responding positively in love.

CONTROLLING NEGATIVE EMOTIONS

We inspire them to no longer be driven to react negatively in fear but to respond positively in love. Realizing that as they respond in love, they create a positive, united environment for all. Being inspired that all feel fulfilled when the environment changes to a positive one.

Rather than allowing their sensibilities to disqualify them, they are inspired to use them to help others uniquely. Seeing their uniqueness inspires them to see how worthy they are to help others and how much they have to give them. Being inspired to think about others' needs more than their own helps them overcome their self-rejection or disqualification.

We inspire others to see how their unique abilities can help others, and this inspires them to give even more of themselves to others instead of being so hypersensitive that they withdraw in fear. Inspiring them to respond positively to people who may have triggered fearful memories causes them to withdraw in fear, as they would overreact to them.

These breakthroughs allow them to be no longer controlled by negative emotions. Still, they are inspired to respond from a place of positive emotions and wait and think about their response before overreacting because of being hypersensitive. Instead of allowing others to torment them, they are inspired to control their negative emotions and be at peace. By responding peacefully, they no longer allow others to torment them. This knowledge about themselves inspires them to no longer let others torment them through their actions or reactions toward them. By becoming good listeners, they can respond positively instead of negatively to others they fear. Through being good listeners, they are inspired to respond to the needs of others with wisdom and sensitivity. Their sensitivity causes them to act wisely and gently, which draws others to them and enables them to work together in greater harmony.

As they are inspired to work together in harmony with others, they can see their potential and uniqueness, sharing it freely without fear. They are inspired by the reactions of others, enabling them to open up to them instead of withdrawing from them. The more they open up to others and work with them, the easier they find it to be sincere, vulnerable, and transparent with them. People are likelier to open up and be humble when they sense their genuine sensitivity, care, and concern. They inspire others by showing mutual humility and respect as they work harmoniously.

By developing strong relationships with others, they can understand the power of the word no. Understanding the power of the word no causes us not to overreact when others say no. Saying no without fear allows them to be more sensitive and discerning of the needs of others and others of their needs. Their sensitivity to the needs of others inspires them to serve them instead of withdrawing in fear, as we used to do. Their inspiration to step out and serve others gives them greater fulfillment and joy. Their satisfaction inspires them to serve others more and enjoy what they are doing instead of being fearful of doing it.

CONCLUSION

Instead of being overly sensitive about my disability, I redirected my sensitivity to better understand the needs of those around me. When entering a group of people, I would want to withdraw from in fear, making a willful choice to draw closer to them. Instead of quickly judging them and overeating, I step back and wait. By waiting, I often realize they are not reacting negatively towards me, but my hypersensitivity tried to trick me into thinking they were. This breakthrough was huge for me and has allowed me to develop so many positive friendships with people worldwide that I wouldn't have been open to if I had not recognized and mastered this challenge. Turning my sensitivity outwardly to help others instead of turning it inward has allowed me to inspire and help people of all ages.

APPLICATION

1. What group or groups trigger your sensitivity most?

2. How are you going to change your response to them after this chapter?

3. How can your sensitivity be used negatively or positively?

4. What helps us to not react in fear?

5. What benefits do we enjoy when serving others with genuine, caring compassion?

CHAPTER NINETEEN
THE CHALLENGE OF
BEING DISTANT

My hands were sweating, my mouth was dry, and I was in fear sitting at the back of the class. Why was I feeling this way? It was English class, and it was my turn to stand up and do an oral. I didn't enjoy speaking to my classmates, so I avoided it. Why was I so fearful of getting up to speak? As they had mocked and belittled my slow speech so often in the past, it had made me afraid of their reactions when I had to talk in front of them, even though I had no control over my slow speech because of my cerebral palsy. I responded to their adverse reactions by withholding what I had to offer them or staying quiet when I should have gotten involved. Fear and selfishness made me avoid public speaking and interacting with unfamiliar groups. My selfishness caused me to speak as little as possible, procrastinate, or hold out as long as possible, hoping I could avoid having to speak publicly. My selfish behavior robbed others of what I should have given them and made me lose many valuable opportunities to contribute what I had to contribute.

BREAKDOWN

DISTANCING OURSELVES FROM OTHERS

We become selfish and anxious, lacking confidence, and give in to the fear of failure. We become double-minded, battling to get motivated, lacking vision and purpose. We become hopeless, undervaluing our capabilities.

240

FEAR AND INSECURITY

We become so fearful we find ourselves paralyzed not wanting to interact with others around us. The longer we remain trapped and paralyzed, the more we allow our thinking to be negatively impacted. Our negative thinking then leads to a victim mentality.

LACK VISION AND PURPOSE

Our fear-driven victim mentality results in us procrastinating and withdrawing to try to escape reality. Procrastination and withdrawal result in hopelessness and a lack of vision and purpose. Not finding the right voices to empower us to change, we remain stuck.

When we become too self-centered, we start distancing ourselves from others and not having care or concern for others. Our wrong perceptions of ourselves and others make us focus on the bad things in life, being too self-absorbed. Our self-absorption makes us focus so much on our disabilities we become blinded to our capabilities. Instead of choosing to celebrate our unique differences, we reject or despise them.

We become nervous and scared around unfamiliar people because of our wrong perceptions about ourselves and how they may respond to us. This driving fear makes us distance ourselves from doing things that could expose our weaknesses or disability. Our fears and incorrect perceptions of ourselves and others make us struggle to be bold and confident, often robbing us of being able to do our best. We feel afraid and struggle to be optimistic because we believe we are going to be judged for our weaknesses or disabilities.

The longer we dwell on the wrong things, the more we allow that negativity to torment or paralyze us, making us feel we are not good enough.

Thinking about what torments us instead of our memories leads to a wrong mindset about ourselves and other's perceptions of us. Our negative thinking causes us to see our disability as a disadvantage instead of a strength to help others. We develop a victim mentality because of our negative mindset and see ourselves as victims instead of victorious.

Throughout the book, we have discussed how our challenges can quickly lead us to develop a victim mindset. When we become selfish and do not deal with our victim mentality, we feel insecure and inadequate even when we have much good to offer others. Our victim mentality causes us to struggle to push past our fears, resulting in us experiencing guilt, shame, and other negative emotions. These negative emotions lead to us becoming tormented by guilt and lies, making us fearful of exposing our weaknesses. Our fears then further rob us of our ability to be bold and confident enough to function within our strengths. Robbed by our wrong mentality and worries, we become so blinded to what we can do well that we do not desire even to try to function as we should.

The longer we stay trapped in our wrong mentality, the longer we lack the courage and confidence to move forward. By not moving forward as we should, we become so paranoid that fear takes over and can eventually paralyze us. Our wrong mindset and paranoia cause us to disqualify ourselves even before others see what we have to give them.

We disqualify ourselves before attempting to do the things we should or are required to do, which causes stagnation instead of growth. We then find ourselves stuck in our victim mindset, which keeps us distant from others instead of fully participating with them as we should.

By selfishly distancing ourselves from others, we do not face reality, often going backward instead of progressing forward. We ignore our selfishness and live in an alternate reality, causing us to feel uneasy, paranoid, and distant from others. We feel unstable and distant because we fear how people will react to us. Our paranoia and distance from others make it harder and harder for us to get started or do what we need to do.

Instead of taking a risk and doing our best by selfishly distancing ourselves from others, we find ourselves stuck and held back by procrastination. The longer we delay and procrastinate, the more room we give to our doubts, fears, and shame, further feeding our victim mentality. Instead of starting and focusing on the unique things we can accomplish, we think about past failures and become stuck. Finding ourselves unwilling to ask ourselves the right questions to be able to master our challenge because we've become too focused on ourselves. Rather than asking, "What can I improve on, and what strengths could I embrace to be more effective this time?" We need to be willing to ask questions like this to improve our confidence and passion.

We must gain self-confidence and seek help from coaches or teachers to improve ourselves. Without being equipped, we find ourselves running from our challenges instead of mastering them. Thinking we won't have to deal with them if we hide long enough and remain distanced from them. By running, hiding, and distancing ourselves from our challenges, we believe we will not have to deal with them.

However, that is not true. It just delays what eventually will have to be done. Instead of seeking help from mentors or coaches to deal with our challenges effectively, we withdraw and pretend nothing is wrong. Allowing our fears and paranoia to defeat our dreams and hopes instead of seeking help and encouragement. Isolation leads to negative self-talk, making it difficult to hear and obey the positive voices we should be listening to and obeying.

The longer we remain distant and listen to the wrong voices, the more hopeless we become. The longer we stay tuned into the bad voices and are unwilling to listen to the right ones, the harder it is for us to master being distant from others. Instead of being able to master our challenge with the help of others before it's too late, we find ourselves stuck in our hopelessness.

Our hopelessness hinders us from getting the right help from others with the necessary tools. The longer we remain distant from others, the harder it becomes to overcome our selfishness. Our selfishness and lack of hope rob us of vision for the future. Our lack of hope and vision restricts us from having positive dreams about our future as we should. Our hopelessness and lack of goals make us want to give up and not try to do our best with what we have.

We give up thinking to ourselves selfishly: "I have nothing of value to contribute. How can I help anyone else?" Our selfish thinking and withdrawal from reality cause us not to desire to get engaged or participate as we should. We constantly withdraw when we should advance and move forward to give what we have because of our lack of desire and drive.

Therefore, we do not seek the right people to equip and help us overcome our lack of hope, vision, and drive. When I first sensed and knew I would travel and teach people, I immediately responded, "No, I could never do that. People find it amusing and ridicule me when I speak in public." I would not be writing this book if I had remained stuck listening to those disqualifying voices. We fail when we listen to negative voices inside and let them hold us back instead of listening to the positive ones that can guide us to our true selves. Moving forward and advancing requires us to develop the right mindset and listen to the correct voices. When we dwell on the wrong voices and things, we distance ourselves from those who can help us hear the right voices and ignore those trying to support us.

BREAKTHROUGH

PAUSING BEFORE REACTING

Stop being selfish and anxious. Be bold and confident, and give what you have without fear of failure. By being single-focused on what we should be doing, we have a definite vision and purpose, which gives us hope.

RELEASE FEAR AND INSECURITY

Recognizing what tries to paralyze us stops us from interacting positively with others as we should. We no longer allow ourselves to remain trapped and paralyzed by negative thinking. But instead, developing a positive way of thinking, which destroys our victim mentality.

PROGRESS WITH VISION AND PURPOSE

As our mentality changes, we gain vision and purpose. We no longer withdraw from procrastination but advance with hope, vision, and purpose. We surround ourselves with empowering voices who encourage us to move on in victory as overcomers.

Be filled with hope, valuing our capabilities, and advancing with the help of others close to us. We master breaking through our challenge of distancing ourselves from others by being aware of our negative feelings and choosing to respond positively to the needs of others rather than distancing ourselves from them. Instead of overreacting because of our negative perceptions of others and how they may have responded to us, we wait before quickly overreacting.

By waiting, we can check our motives and think more about other's needs, putting them before our own. Focusing on our strengths and abilities allows us to help others and avoid dwelling on weaknesses and fear of failure. No longer selfishly concentrate on ourselves, saying, "How will they react?" But instead, asking, "What can I do to help meet their need?" We choose not to let others' opinions affect our behavior and how we respond. Preventing us from reacting negatively by doing nothing, we do our best to meet their needs and push past our fears. When we respond positively, we celebrate and embrace our uniqueness instead of rejecting our value and worth. As we celebrate and embrace who we are, we become bolder and more confident in who we are and what we must give to those we contact daily.

Our confidence removes our fear and helps us change to focus on our strengths rather than our weaknesses. Seeing our strengths as more significant than our weaknesses and failures gives us greater confidence to offer what we have to others. We no longer allow them to torment us, but we will enable them to encourage us as we embrace them as we should. Instead of despising them, by adopting and learning from them, we discover some of our greatest life lessons through them. Look how many life lessons you have benefited from through this book, as I have transparently and openly discussed my challenges. I was challenged to see the good in challenges instead of dwelling on the bad, which changed my life. Recognizing the value of our weaknesses and failures can change our mindset and prevent a victim mentality.

We master our victim mentality by not allowing it to grow or get a foothold in our minds. Instead, we think about ourselves differently, seeing ourselves as so unique no one else can give what we have been given through our uniqueness. I can uniquely help others; if I don't, someone else might, and we will miss out on the opportunity I had. Realizing that I may have lost my chance by remaining distant and not giving what I should have given us from someone else should motivate me to break free of my procrastination.

Being motivated by these realities of lost opportunities should cause us to push past our tormenting fears and feel shame for not giving what we should have given. Having the correct motivation makes us listen to the truth rather than the lies that try to disqualify us and have us paralyzed by fear. Rather than being paralyzed by fear, we choose to be motivated by a caring concern to give what we alone can give to others. We don't let ourselves stay in a victim mentality. Instead, our loving nature drives us to boldly and courageously reach out to others in need. We aim to give our best and work on our weaknesses instead of letting them disqualify us.

Our willingness to give of our strengths and abilities breaks our cycle of stagnation. Therefore, rather than stagnating, we try new things, allowing ourselves to be stretched and grow. As we grow and break free of our selfish limitations, we find joy and a sense of fulfillment, value, and worth in no longer feeling trapped and bound by our fears. Our growth leads us to recognize our ability to give to others, and we become more engaged instead of withdrawing from those in need.

By pushing past our selfish fears which want to hold us back, we break free to give what we should be to others. Seeing positive things happen when we stop being distant and selfishly motivates us to get involved in helping others. Positive feedback from them helps us stay on track. Seeing our disability or disabilities serves as a breakthrough from our distant, selfish behavior. Growing up, I was super sensitive; therefore, I reacted to frights more than most. My overreaction to others made them do it even more, as it was so much fun frightening me and seeing my reactions. My cerebral palsy made me extra sensitive to how people reacted to my weaknesses in school and public life.

OVERCOMING REJECTION

As you've heard me say before, one thing I struggled with was being able to write as quickly as my fellow students could. I felt ashamed and hurt when others mocked me for my slow writing because of cerebral palsy. However, I learned to accept that I could only do my best and chose not to react or get upset with others or myself. During the challenge of self-acceptance, I mentioned when a student called me spaz while I was taking notes from the overhead projector in biology class. Instead of reacting, I did the best I could. As I explained in the challenge of being hypersensitive, I had to learn not to put up my walls and choose to shut down if kids started laughing when I began talking. I was often over-sensitive to others when they were not laughing at me. And even if they were, I could do nothing to change my slow speech because of my cerebral palsy.

I had to choose not to see myself as a victim but as a victor by focusing on responding positively rather than negatively. I began working on my weaknesses and asking what value I and others could get from them being used positively. I value my past failures because they taught me important life lessons that I can share with others. Instead of allowing past paranoia and fear to paralyze and hold me back, I learned to allow it to propel me forward positively. Instead of hiding and trying to live in unreality, I began boldly and courageously seeking how I could get out and help others. As I did so, I started seeking and receiving positive dreams and visions, giving me incredible hope for my future and what I would pursue.

When we face rejection, we can overcome our fears and negativity by focusing on our dreams and visions instead of our weaknesses. Our passion for what we should be doing helps our dreams and visions become a reality. Our passion also deals a death blow to procrastination, which wants to prevent us from doing what we should be doing to see our dreams and visions fulfilled. Our passion brings us joy and hope, and we stop feeling hopeless. We inquire about ways to overcome our weaknesses and improve our disability. We no longer let shyness hold us back but instead embrace our uniqueness with a newfound passion, desiring to use our abilities and capabilities to become bolder and grow in confidence.

INSPIRE

REFOCUSING ON STRENGTHS

Not focusing on their weaknesses or disabilities, feeling like an overcomer, not a victim. Learning to focus on what they can do without being distant and fearful.

DEVELOPING A NEW BELIEF SYSTEM

Developing a new belief system that values their past mistakes. Becoming aware of the negative feelings that want to bring distance between them and others. Choosing to respond positively. Training themselves not to overreact.

LEARN THE ART OF WAITING

Instead of overeating, they are inspired to patiently wait before overreacting negatively. By waiting, they can check their motives and think about others' needs instead of their own. Focusing on their strengths allows them to help others and not discard their weaknesses or fears of failure.

Their new focus inspires them to stop selfishly focusing on themselves and being hypersensitive to how others may react to them. Instead, they are inspired to ask themselves, "What can I do to help meet the needs of others around me?" Their correct focus inspires them not to let others' opinions affect their behavior and response. Not focusing on others' reactions prevents them from reacting negatively by distancing themselves and doing nothing; instead, they do their best to meet others' needs, pushing past their fears.

Their positive response inspires them to celebrate and embrace their uniqueness instead of rejecting their value and worth. Celebrating and embracing who they are makes them bolder and more confident. Their confidence replaces their fear and inspires them to change from focusing on their strengths, not their weaknesses. Seeing their strengths as more significant than their weaknesses and failures inspires them to become far more confident to offer what they have to others instead of distancing themselves from them.

Their confidence replaces their torment, encouraging them to embrace and celebrate their uniqueness as they should. They are inspired to embrace and learn from their weaknesses, turning them into their most significant life lessons for themselves and others to learn from. Just as you have benefited from and been inspired by the life lessons, I have discussed with you through this book. They are inspired by the truth that transparency and openness will draw them closer to others instead of distancing them from others in fear.

Their transparency inspires them to see the good in their challenges instead of dwelling on the bad, knowing they could change their lives. Recognizing the value of their weaknesses and failures changes their mindset and prevents a victim mentality from developing within them.

They are inspired to master their victim mentality by not allowing it to grow or get a foothold in their minds. By thinking positively about themselves differently and seeing themselves as unique, no one else can give what they have been given through their uniqueness. Realizing they can uniquely help others, and if they don't, someone else might, and they will miss out on the opportunity they could have had. Realizing that they may have lost their chance by remaining distant and not giving what they should have given to others inspires them to break free of any procrastination.

Being motivated by these realities of lost opportunities should inspire them to push past their tormenting fears and shame for not giving what they should have given. Having the correct motivation inspires them to listen to the truth rather than the lies trying to disqualify and paralyze them with fear. Rather than being paralyzed by fear, they choose to be motivated by a caring concern to give what they can to others. Their positive inspiration frees them from living in a victim mentality to living as a victor. Their inspiration and caring nature cause them to boldly and courageously reach out to others in need instead of standing far from them. They are inspired to give their best and work on their weaknesses instead of letting their weaknesses disqualify them. Their willingness to give of their strengths and abilities frees them from being stuck at a distance from others in stagnation. Therefore, rather than stagnating, they are inspired to try new things, allowing themselves to be stretched and grow through being pushed beyond their comfort zones.

As they grow and become free of their selfish limitations, which want to keep them at a distance from others, they find joy and a sense of fulfillment, value, and worth in no longer feeling trapped and bound by their fears. Their growth leads them to recognize how much potential they have within themselves to give to others, inspiring them to get fully engaged instead of withdrawing from those in need.

By being inspired to push past their selfish fears holding them back, they break free by giving what they should to others rather than distancing themselves from them. The positive things that begin happening when they stop selfishly distancing themselves inspire them to get involved in helping others. Inspired by the positive feedback from those they have reached out to, they stay on track and keep giving more of themselves to others. Inspired by how their disability or disabilities can serve others, it frees them from their distant, selfish behavior. Instead of being negatively super-sensitive and overreacting, they are inspired and at peace with changing what they can and not losing their passion to serve others.

They are inspired to overcome their fears and negativity by focusing on their positive dreams and visions instead of being trapped by their weaknesses. Their passion for what they should be doing helps their dreams and visions become a reality. Their newfound passion also deals a death blow to procrastination, which prevents them from doing what they should be doing to fulfill their dreams and visions. Their passion brings them joy and hope, and giving them hope. They are inspired to seek positive ways to overcome their weaknesses and improve their disability. Through their victory, they no longer let shyness hold them back but instead embrace their uniqueness passionately, desiring to use their abilities and capabilities to become bolder and grow in their self-confidence.

CONCLUSION

After seeing how much joy it brought me when I forced myself not to distance myself from others selfishly, I began choosing to do it more and more. The more I did it, the easier it became for me to do it, instead of negatively focusing on my stumbling blocks {weaknesses or seeming inabilities} and allowing them to close my eyes to my true value, worth, and ability. Instead, I began focusing on how what I saw as stumbling blocks {weaknesses or seeming inabilities} could be used as building blocks to help others as I made myself available to help them. This mindset change brought me closer to others than ever before and filled me with a passion, zeal, and joy that has kept me going.

One of my great heroes is Nick Vujicic. Nick is a man with no arms and no legs, yet what he has and is achieving remarkably. His story has touched millions of people all around the world. He swims, plays sports, sails, and surfs. His life included writing books, getting married, and having children. Without fear, he freely talks about his weaknesses or what people would call his disability of having no limbs. He has had such a positive, victorious mindset that he only sees his abilities using them as boldly as possible. He focuses on his abilities, not his inabilities, which inspire others to live life to the fullest.[13]

---

[13] Limbs, L. W. (2024b, May 1). Home - NickV Ministries. NickV Ministries. https://nickvministries.org/

APPLICATION

1. How has your challenge of distancing yourself from others prevented you from sharing what you uniquely have?

2. How do you react when you meet someone who reminds you of a past hurt?

3. What can you change to see yourself differently?

4. What should you do about things you cannot change as they are part of your life?

5. How do you change from being a victim to becoming a victorious overcomer?

CHAPTER TWENTY
THE CHALLENGE OF PERFECTIONISM

"Why did you get so angry with the person who had taken the time to put together that three-ring binder for you?"

Someone asked me this. At first, our question started making me step back and think about it. As I did, I realized that if someone I'd asked to do something for me did not do it perfectly, I would get furious. Why? As I sought to dig deeper, I was willing to continue. The answer revealed that rejected people strive to be perfectionists as they fear rejection if

They need to do things perfectly, and they fear rejection if they cannot do something perfectly when asked to. Thus, the fear of rejection leads them to respond incorrectly and can eventually lead to prideful tendencies.

BREAKDOWN

BATTLE TO DELEGATE

Therefore, we feel overwhelmed by unnecessary burdens. We get impatient, frustrated, dishonor others, and angry with them. We are unable to differentiate between stewardship, excellence, and perfectionism.

BECOMING ANGRY

Finally, lashing out in anger which startles others unaware of our frustration and weariness. As they are unaware of our fear of rejection and perfectionism.

FEELING CHALLENGED AND INSECURE

We struggle with people who excel. We feel insecure when they do something better than we can. We struggle to delegate, fearing rejection if they don't do a perfect job. We do not want to say no, as we may be rejected if we do.

Carrying false responsibilities makes us exhausted and feel overwhelmed with all that needs to be done or by the needs around us. By lacking boundaries and being unable to say no, we become overly tired and feel burnout. Our exhaustion and burnout lead to negative behaviors and attitudes growing within us. As these negative behaviors and attitudes surface, we become impatient and lack the peace we should have. Our agitation frustrates us when others don't meet our unrealistic standards, making us angry with them. If we don't recognize and address our frustration soon enough, we will begin disrespecting through our frustration and anger.

When we struggle with being perfectionists, we struggle with people being able to do this as well as we can or better than we can, causing two significant problems. First, we do not want to give a task to someone else to do if they can do it better than we can as we subconsciously think, if they do it better than me, I may not be needed anymore. As I mentioned in the performance challenge, rejected or challenged, people battle with a need to be needed, often getting their self-worth from what they are doing instead of who they are, which drives perfectionists.

Secondly, because of their insecurities, those driven to be perfectionists do not want to acknowledge that anyone else has done anything as well as they can or better than they can. Therefore, they need help recognizing when someone has done an excellent job and complimenting them when they should. They find it hard to say, "Well done, you did a great job and accomplished what you needed to do." Instead, they will raise the bar and make it harder for the person to achieve what needs to be completed. It is most destructive in family relationships when a child tries as hard as they can to achieve a goal, and instead of the parent saying, "Well done," they set a higher standard for them. Earlier in our journey, I mentioned that the young lady tried her best to get straight A's to please her father. Instead of complimenting her for her achievement, he said, "I'm sorry college is so easy." His reaction destroyed her, and she became a prostitute. In the business world, instead of complimenting workers for their excellent achievements, their bosses often raise the bar, telling them to achieve more.

Raising the bar causes them to become so discouraged they lose motivation and frequently quit their jobs. The root behind people not being willing to compliment others as they should is pride, as they are not willing to humble themselves and acknowledge the person has done as well or better than they could do. We need to guard against this happening and always be willing to compliment others for their achievements.

We struggle with these opposing challenges, lacking a breakthrough as we look at things through our rejection lenses instead of lenses of self-acceptance, which is again linked to the challenge of disdain we addressed in the previous section of this book. People who can't distinguish between perfectionism, excellence, and stewardship struggle with perfectionism.

Therefore, we are driven to achieve perfectionism instead of being led to do things excellently with all our heart and soul. We are unwilling to let ourselves or others grow from our mistakes, but we try extra hard not to make mistakes, desiring to succeed and do what we do perfectly. We become poor losers as we strive to be the top dog, fearing rejection or being looked down upon if we don't win by always being the top dog. Our aggression pushes people away, making it harder for us to get help when needed. It makes it harder for us to get others to work with or help us. Achieving a perfectionist's standard means we will set a higher one instead of congratulating others for their achievements, often resulting in us giving up and not wanting to continue with what we should be doing.

BREAKTHROUGH

RECOGNIZING PERFECTIONISTIC WAYS

Learning to delegate tasks to others rather than try to do everything perfectly ourselves. Knowing when we are starting to feel overwhelmed, overburdened, or burned out by what we are doing.

HAVING THE COURAGE TO SAY NO

We are willing to tell others to carry what they need without fear. We set clear, necessary boundaries. Freeing ourselves from carrying others' burdens. We feel relaxed, at peace, and joyful, which is reflected in our behavior.

We break through being caught in this challenge of perfectionism by choosing to delegate what we should to others; we can trust to do what we need to do. Breaking through our negative thinking, will I be rejected if I delegate this task to them and they do not complete it perfectly? By saying, "How can I help them do it correctly next time if they do not do what I have asked them to do well?" We make the right choices not to allow our fear of rejection to cause us to hesitate to delegate the tasks we need to delegate to others.

As others begin carrying what they need to carry and we only carry what we should, we feel lighter and can function as we should without feeling weighed down and heavy. Feeling lighter by choosing to do what we should be doing allows us to recognize what tasks we need to say yes or no.

Our discernment gives us the courage to tell others to carry what they need without fear of rejection. We set the boundaries necessary to free ourselves from taking on the burdens others should carry and be responsible for. As we are no longer willing to carry others' burdens or responsibilities, we are no longer overly tired or feeling burnout. Instead, we feel relaxed, at peace, and joyful, positively impacting our behavior toward those around us.

Our peaceful state replaces our agitation and frustration when others don't meet our unrealistic standards, and rather than getting angry with them, we choose to help them be better at what they do for themselves or us. Our peaceful joy replacing our frustration and anger causes us to be respectful to others instead of getting frustrated and angry with them. Our breakthrough causes all of our relationships to be strengthened and enriched rather than causes them to be bewildered by our adverse reactions toward them.

We break through our struggle with perfectionism by being at peace with people being able to do this as well as we can or better than we can. Being at peace breaks down two significant problems when we always try to be the top dog. First, we willingly give tasks to others, especially if we see that they can do it better than we can. Knowing that if they did it better than me, we could be free to do what I could do better than them without having to make it a competition.

In this way, we fight against our challenge to try to outperform others and choose to work in unity with them. Knowing we each have unique areas of expertise; we can function in giving our best. Being aware of the truth that what we do is not who we are; it's how we function. By acknowledging this, we stop being driven or driving ourselves and begin being led and stopping ourselves whenever we feel driven. Secondly, instead of allowing our insecurities to drive us and not celebrate others' achievements, we consciously acknowledge and celebrate their achievements, especially when they have done something better than we could do. Therefore, they need help recognizing when someone has done an excellent job and complimenting them when they should.

Often saying, "Well done, you did a great job and accomplished what you needed to do." Instead of simply raising the bar and making it harder for them to achieve what needs to be completed, we keep it at the same level and encourage them to keep up the excellent work. In our family relationships, when a child tries as hard to achieve a goal set for them, we celebrate their achievement with joy—being humble enough to acknowledge when they have done a job as well as us or better than us. Doing this encourages our children and others to be motivated to keep going and excel at what they are good at.

We break through our feelings of exhaustion by stopping and asking ourselves the hard questions we need to. Such as "What am I able to do with excellence, and what should I be delegating to others to do?" Why am I not willing to delegate what I should be delegating to others around me who should be helping me share my load?" As we wait and listen, working through our answers honestly and maturely, we discern our responsibility and reasons for not delegating to others.

Knowing what we are responsible for and what we are supposed to carry stimulates us to begin doing it instead of staying stuck in our overwhelmed feelings. Knowing what we are to delegate to others gives us the courage to do so without fearing they may reject us for doing so. Rather than being hesitant about their ability to do what we've asked them to with excellence, we decide if they don't do it as well as they should, we can train and equip them to do it better next time.

THE CHALLENGE OF PERFECTIONISM

Our courage to delegate, as we should, releases us from taking on false burdens or responsibilities that are not ours to carry and be burdened with. Our release from false burdens and responsibilities enables us to function correctly and feel refreshed and excited about what we must do instead of overly exhausted. We find a new boldness, allowing us to say no to what is not our responsibility, making us most effective at what we can do well.

Functioning from a place of rest makes us patient, peaceful, and caring toward others. We are willing to teach them how to do what they need to do correctly and better the next time they try. As we teach them, we do so calmly with the right motivation, not in anger, irritation, or frustration, as was our tendency before our breakthrough. By not losing our relaxation and starting them, we enrich their lives and help them improve at what they do, eventually excellently.

By being in the right mind, we can lead others instead of being driven or driving others. Quickly identify when we are being driven versus being led, which impacts our interactions with others, giving them an example to follow. Instead of becoming angry with ourselves or others for not doing something perfectly, we are willing to learn how to do it excellently or to show others how to do what we need to, teaching others the correct stewardship principles.

We break through our perfectionistic ways or challenges by setting attainable standards for ourselves, our children, and others. We celebrate when they have achieved a set goal or done a task excellently and allow them to celebrate us for our achievements. By celebrating one another's achievements, we begin to honor and respect each other as we should, breaking the negative cycle of dishonoring or disrespecting each other.

As we grow in our ability to celebrate each other, we soon find that it replaces our anger and hash ways. Instead of driving others to do things perfectly, we encourage them to do their best with passion and dedication. Instead of harshly criticizing them for not doing something perfectly, we take the time needed to help them improve their performance by pointing out their errors and showing them how to do what they are doing with excellence. With our help, they can become better stewards and achieve more excellence in the future. Coming to see that often, the best way to learn is through practical experience and learning from their mistakes. The most painful life lessons are the ones we value most, even though it's not a pleasant experience to walk through them and be humble enough to acknowledge we needed help in that area. It left the most lasting impact on my life, even though it was unpleasant when I went through us.

INSPIRE

LEARNING TO DELEGATE

Inspiring them to share and delegate tasks to others rather than try to do everything perfectly themselves. Know when they start feeling overwhelmed, overburdened, or burned out by what they are doing.

THINKING THROUGH THINGS

We inspire others to allow themselves time to think through what they are to do, to boldly know what to say yes to. Allowing them to conserve their energy rather than having it sapped from them.

WORK FROM A PLACE OF REST

We inspire them to know when they need to rest and find peace within. Inspiring them to embrace their mistakes and allow themselves and others to learn valuable lessons from them.

We inspire others through our victories over perfectionism to prioritize delegating tasks they are incapable of doing or have the time to do to others who can and have the time to do them. Their willingness to delegate inspires them to share their load with those qualified to do what needs to be done. They use how they feel about doing things assigned to them to gauge what should be pursued and what they should allow others to do. Inspired by their knowledge of what they need to delegate, they are prevented from becoming overburdened by taking on responsibilities that are not theirs.

They are inspired to allow themselves to take the necessary time to think through what they are to be doing and be comfortable with doing it before committing to doing it. Their discernment enables them to boldly know what to say yes to, not simply say yes to everything but what to say no to. Asking themselves, "Would doing that be the best use of my unique abilities and capabilities? Will it give me energy or take energy from me? Will that be the best use of my time?" Their willingness to ask these questions before committing themselves inspires them to be diligent and wise about what they do and say yes to doing. It also helps them to allow what they do to conserve their energy rather than sapping it.

They find themselves inspired to know their unique skills and qualifications and how to use them to help others most wisely. Being inspired to conserve their energy enables them to prioritize their efforts and no longer constantly feel tired or weary. By being selective in their energy expenditure, they feel motivated to do an excellent job and enjoy their work. Being inspired to work from a place of rest patiently, peacefully, and carefully brings joy to them and those around them, positively changing their atmosphere.

Even when facing the most complex challenges, they find themselves inspired to keep calm and respond correctly in honorable, respectful ways. Inspiring them to help and encourage others when they have not done a job as well as they should have and take the time to show them how to do it better the next time. Their inspiration to choose to help others replaces their tendency to get frustrated and angry.

Their inspiration and willingness to help others do a better job draws others to them instead of driving them away, as they are never sure when they may explode. Inspired by what happens and the positive results of being patient and waiting, they are inspired to take the time needed to encourage and celebrate others' achievements without simply rushing to get their job done. By taking this time to help others, they see others equipped and able to improve their work. Their uniqueness inspires them so much that they no longer feel driven to do everything and do it better than anyone else. Therefore, they are inspired to delegate even more tasks to others. Knowing that if what they have delegated to others is not done correctly, they have an excellent opportunity to show them how to do it better the next time. Inspiring them to embrace and celebrate their mistakes and the mistakes of others shows how many valuable life lessons can be gained from them.

They are inspired not to take things too personally, becoming overly defensive and unteachable when others show them how to do something better. Instead, they are inspired to celebrate being able to do what they need to with more outstanding excellence in the future. Their joy at being celebrated inspires them to celebrate others, creating a positive chain reaction that profoundly affects their environment. Instead of being driven by their fear of rejection, if they or others don't do things perfectly, they are led by a peaceful joy.

Their calm, joy-filled environment replaces their previous environment, which was filled with tolerance, frustration, anger, and strife. Their positive environment inspires those working with them and helps them become better stewards willing to learn from and be celebrated by those around them. This positive atmosphere inspires them to honor and respect others instead of constantly dishonoring and disrespecting them for not doing their job well enough. They are inspired to encourage others and distinguish between responsibility and excellence without pushing for perfectionism. Being freed from constantly having to be the top dog, but celebrating others who do well and help them be the top dogs.

CONCLUSION

Throughout this book, we have been on the journey to recognize strategic challenges faced by ourselves and those around us we come in contact with daily. I have shown you the journey I have been on and am still learning lessons from, as I am willing to ask myself hard questions when I encounter a challenge I do not understand. When someone challenged me to see the positive things in my life, not just the negative ones resulting from rejection, I had a breakthrough over being a victim. Are you willing to do that for yourself and those you come in contact with that you may not have understood? So many need your life lessons and what you have gained from our journey together. Please share us with others. Thank you for being on the journey with you, and safe travels ahead.

APPLICATION

1. Do you get angry with yourself when you don't do things perfectly?

2. Do you get angry with others when they don't do things perfectly?

3. What tasks do you find hardest to delegate to others?

4. What do you see as the difference between excellence and perfectionism?

5. How easy do you find it to celebrate others' achievements?